W . Jackson.

THE DOWNFALL OF TURKEY

AND THE

RETURN OF THE TEN TRIBES.

May 1984 'ORLO' #169 ƒ 10,000

THE

PREDICTED DOWNFALL

OF

THE TURKISH POWER

THE

PREPARATION FOR THE RETURN
OF THE TEN TRIBES.

BY

G. S. FABER, B.D.

MASTER OF SHERBURN HOSPITAL AND PREBENDARY OF SALISBURY.

Ἐν τῇδ ἔφασκε γῇ· τὸ δὲ ζητούμενον,
Ἁλωτὸν· ἐκφεύγει δὲ τἀμελούμενον.
ŒDIP. *Tyran.* 110, 111.

Second Edition,

WITH AN APPENDIX AND OTHER ADDITIONS.

LONDON :

THOMAS BOSWORTH, 215 REGENT STREET.

—

MDCCCLIII.

LONDON:
Printed by G. BARCLAY, Castle St. Leicester Sq.

PREFACE.

THE utility of a Preface very much consists in briefly giving a clear idea of the subject about to be discussed, and in thus preventing any misapprehension.

Under such an aspect, a Preface may not seem quite out of place, even as respects so small a Production as the present.

I. With our best commentators, I consider the Downfall of the Ottoman Power to be clearly predicted in Scripture. Hence, whenever the destined time shall arrive, all the complications of modern political diplomacy will be found totally unable to prevent the Ruin of that once formidable Empire.

But, though its downfall is thus, I think,

absolutely certain, we have no warrant for specifying any precise year.

In general, we know from Prophecy, that its Dissolution *must* occur *before* the Close of the 1260 years and *before* the Commencement of the Time of the End.

This knowledge, *in the abstract*, we possess: and we should also possess it *in the concrete*, if we knew with certainty the exact time when the 1260 years will expire.

There is great reason to believe, that they will expire in the year 1864.

Whence, if this opinion be correct, the Ottoman Power *must* fall some time before the arrival of that year. But we cannot be absolutely certain that it *is* correct.

This, indeed, we know, that that grand period cannot *as yet* have elapsed, because Daniel teaches us, that its Close will be marked by the commencing restoration of his People*. And we

* Dan. xii. 1, 6, 7.

further know, from other prophecies, that his
People comprehends both the Israelites of the
Ten Tribes and the proper Jews of the Two
Tribes : because they are described, as being converted and restored simultaneously and unitedly ;
so that, in future, they shall constitute, as of
old, a single people*.

Now it is quite clear, that this has not yet
been accomplished.

Therefore it plainly follows, that the 1260
years have not yet expired.

II. The Downfall of the Ottoman Power, let
it occur when it may, is a matter of vast scriptural importance.

It will prepare the way for the Return of the
Ten Tribes : and their Return will synchronise
with the Return of the Two Tribes.

We have no right, however, to conclude, that
the Restoration of Israel will *immediately* follow
the Downfall of Turkey. A way will be *prepared*
by the removal of an obstacle : but it does not

* Ezek. xxxvii. 11–28.

therefore follow, that Israel will *instantaneously avail itself* of the preparation.

How long a time will intervene between the two events, we are not enabled to determine. This only we know, that the Downfall of Turkey will occur at the Pouring out of the Sixth Apocalyptic Vial, but that the Restoration of Israel will not take place until the Pouring out of the Seventh Vial.

Here, again, we may be certain *in the abstract*, without being certain *in the concrete*.

III. The Subversion of the Turkish Power will evidently occasion, as all seem to anticipate, a fearful general war.

This war will, I believe, be the last under the present order of things. It will commence, indeed, in Europe : but, at the close of the 1260 years, or at the Pouring out of the Seventh Vial, or at the Commencement of the Time of the End (for these several matters are synchronical), it will pass into Palestine.

IV. Of the progress of the Wilful Roman

King associated with his ally the False Roman Prophet, a wonderfully minute account is given by Daniel.

He will be opposed, it seems, by the two Powers, which at that time will be the lords respectively of Egypt and of Syria : whence those two Powers are called the *King of the South* and the *King of the North*. But the event only can determine with certainty *what* those two Powers will be.

They will, however, according to Daniel, be unable to prevent the progress of the Wilful King, when he invades the glorious land : but, notwithstanding this inability, Edom and Moab and the chief of the children of Ammon, whatever may be the States designated by those ancient names, will escape out of his hand. Nevertheless, Egypt will *not* thus escape : and while he has power over its treasures, the Libyans and the African Cuthim will be at his steps. Yet, when disturbed by tidings out of the East and out of the North, he shall plant the tabernacles of his palaces, between the seas, in the glorious holy mountain, he will, in exact conformity with other parallel prophecies which treat of the same time and the same subject, come to his end, none being able to help him*.

V. When, at the Pouring out of the Sixth Vial, Turkey shall have fallen, the Kings of the whole Roman World, we are told, will be gathered to the war of that great Day of God Almighty.

Thus, plainly, the Downfall of Turkey will be, at once, both the signal and the cause of this terrible war.

The Confederation will be formed by the joint intrigues of what are called *Three Unclean Spirits :* and, by noting the sources whence they had proceeded, we may form no unreasonable conjecture as to their character. Be they what

---

* Dan. xi. 40–45. Compare Isaiah, xi. 10–16; lix. 16–21; lxvi. 5–24 ; Joel, ii. ; Zechar. xii–xiv. ; Rev. xix. 11–21.

they may, they are spirits of *evil*. Whence we may be sure, that the gathering of the Roman Kings infers no *good* purpose.

A general war may clearly, I think, be set down as the consequence of the Downfall of Turkey: and, in the course of its evolutions, Israel will be restored.

As to *particulars,* we must not venture further than Scripture doth, as it were, take us by the hand. Of *this,* however, we may be sure, that THE DOWNFALL OF TURKEY WILL BE THE HARBINGER OF THE RESTORATION OF ISRAEL.

Sherburn House,
June 14, 1853.

DOWNFALL OF THE OTTOMAN POWER,

RETURN OF THE TEN TRIBES.

EVENTS are now succeeding each other with an almost portentous rapidity : and, in point of Prophetic Chronology, we are also concurrently approaching to the Fated time of the End, or the Close of the Latter Three Times and a Half.

This may be safely said in the abstract. But, furthermore, connecting Prophetic Chronology with Secular Chronology, we may additionally say, in the concrete, that there is very great reason to believe, that the Three Times and a Half will expire, and that the brief intermediate period denominated *The Time of the End* and synchronising with the Seventh Apocalyptic Vial will commence, in the year 1864.

The last adjustment cannot be propounded as an absolute certainty : but, so far as I can judge, it contains the highest amount of probability. The question, however, is so fully discussed in

my *Sacred Calendar of Prophecy*, that I would
refer the inquirer to that Work, rather than in-
troduce superfluous repetition into the present
brief Discussion. Suffice it to say, that, although
I have tested that and various other points with
as much unsparing severity as I can command, I
have seen no reason to retract any *essential* position maintained in my *Sacred Calendar*.

I. The revival of the short-lived and sword-
slain Seventh Head of the Roman Empire, or, in
other words, the Revival of the Emperorship of
the French, the duration of which, ere it was cut
down by the sword of foreign war, was so short,
that the governing dynasty consisted at the most
of only two individuals, is the last solemn warning
that has been struck upon the bell of Prophecy :
a warning, the more impressively solemn, because
we are definitely taught, that, under the now
revived Seventh Polity, the guilty apostate Empire is doomed, at the Close of the Three Times
and a Half, or the Twelve Hundred and Sixty
years, to go into utter destruction*.

I mean not rashly to affirm, that its destruction
will occur under the *present* Individual Representative of the revived Seventh Polity. Such

* Rev. xvii. 8, 11.

may, or may not be, the case. But, on *this* point, there is no *anterior* certainty. With very few exceptions, Prophecy treats of Dynasties and Empires, not of mere Individuals who may successively represent such Dynasties or successively administer such Empires : and the acts of the governing Individuals are thence considered, not as their own personal acts, but as the acts of the Empire or Dynasty. On this well-ascertained principle, the Roman Empire, for anything that we *know* to the contrary, *may* be destined to go into destruction *as* an Empire under a totally different Individual from its present Chief.

But, that we *are* now in the last stage of the Empire's progress, cannot, I think, admit of a doubt : because it is now under its predicted Seventh and Last Head, which proves itself to be such by its exact accomplishment of what has been foretold respecting it ; and likewise because, under that very Head in its revived state, it is doomed to perish, not alone, but along with the False Ecclesiastical Prophet*.

II. Of late, various attempts have been made to identify the Seventh Head with *this* Power or with *that* Power : and their several authors,

* Rev. xix. 20.

without (so far as I can perceive) bringing their Schemes to the test of a close examination, claim, with a premature positiveness, to have *each* fully established the truth*.

But, when the test is applied, they invariably break down in some necessary point or other.

1. Thus the Seventh Head has been confidently pronounced to be the Emperorship of Dioclesian and his colleagues, for no better reason, than because in some internal political arrangements it differed from the Roman Emperorship of Augustus: a project about as reasonable, as to pronounce the English Monarchy of William III. an entirely new Kingship altogether distinct from the English Monarchy of the Stuarts or the Tudors, or the Plantagenets.

But mark how it fails, when submitted to the test.

After this mere internal modification of the Roman Basileïs or Emperorship had been succeeded by the sole domination of Constantine, it was never revived. For most idle and quite unsatisfactory it is to say, that the Dioclesianic Emperorship was revived in the Papacy; a Power,

---

* One of these gentlemen literally concludes with, *Quod erat demonstrandum !*

both nominally and circumstantially, different in every respect.

2. Thus, again, with some variation of the preceding theory, the Seventh Head has been confidently pronounced to be Dioclesian and his Colleagues viewed collectively as sustaining the office of what the writer calls *The Diademed Pontifex Maximus*, to whom we must add, as a continuation of this supposed Seventh Head, Constantine and all the Emperors who subsequently bore the same title. How that imagined Head was slain by the sword, the writer does not seem to have quite made up his mind. The prophecy, he thinks, may refer, either to the defeat of Licinius by Constantine, or to the defeat of Julian by the Parthians ; though, by his own shewing, the defeat of neither of these *Pontifices Maximi* produced the death or violent extinction of the Head. But, if such a self-contradictory application should be rejected as unsatisfactory, then we must understand the mortal wound inflicted by the sword, not *literally*, but *figuratively*, as importing the voluntary resignation of the title by Gratian. At all events, however the Head was slain, it ceased for a season to exist in a state of vitality : but, it was revived by the healing of its

B

deadly wound, when the title of *Pontifex Maximus* was assumed by the Pope. Its assumption thus introduced an apparently Eighth Polity : which is never called an *Eighth Head,* because it was really no other than the Seventh Head restored to life by the healing of its deadly sword-inflicted wound.

Such is the present scheme : and, as a proof, I suppose, that this interpretation *must* be correct, we are told, that, to the thus revived Seventh Head, reappearing as a seemingly Eighth Polity, power was given to practise 42 months or 1260 mystical days or 1260 natural years.

The proof, as I understand the argument, lies in this.

The 1260 years are a period, specially predicated of, and appertaining to, the Papacy. But they are also a period, predicated of, and thence appertaining to, the Seventh Head when revived as an Eighth Polity. Therefore, the revived Seventh Head or the Eighth Polity, must be the Papacy.

Here, likewise, mark, how this modification of the former theory fails in every particular.

The character of *Diademed Pontifex Maximus* was NOT that, which constituted Dioclesian with

his pontifical colleagues and successors a Head of
the Roman Empire. Such a supposition is for-
bidden by the vital principle of Homogeneity.
Since History declares the Six First Heads to
have all been *secular,* Homogeneity requires, that
the Seventh Head, both before the reception of
its deadly wound and after its revival by the
healing of that wound, should be *secular* likewise.
But the Pontificate, whether Pagan or Papal, was
strictly *sacerdotal :* for the writer himself states,
that, as the *Pagan Pontifex Maximus* was the
High-Priest of Vesta, so the *Papal Pontifex Maximus* is the High-Priest of the Virgin Mary. At
any rate, the Pontificate, whether Pagan or Papal,
is, confessedly, *sacerdotal,* not *secular.* The plain
consequence, therefore, is : that Dioclesian and
the other *Pagan Pontifices* severally represented a
Roman Head, not as *Sacerdotal Pontifices,* but as
Secular Emperors or Kings the successors of Ro-
mulus and Augustus ; while the *Papal Pontifex,*
as such, was purely *Sacerdotal,* and was NEVER a
Secular Head of the Roman Empire ; for the
temporal sway, over the States of the Church *only,*
could not make the Pope a *Secular Head* of the
Roman Empire.

The writer would make a distinction between

the *Laureated Pontifex Maximus* and the *Diademed Pontifex Maximus*. No doubt, this was necessary to his system. But no such combined title, as either the one or the other, was ever in existence. The title was simply *Pontifex Maximus* : and, if Dioclesian first adopted the Diadem in preference to the Laurel Wreath which distinguished his predecessors, both the Laurel and the Diadem were borne, as the badge of the *Secular Emperorship,* not as the badge of the *Sacerdotal Pontificate*. In truth, the union of the Regality and the Pontifical Priesthood in the same person was nothing more than a relic of primeval antiquity : whence the learnedly archaistic poet Virgil speaks of Anius as being at once a King and the Priest of Phœbus. Nay, the writer himself tells us, that the only difference between what he makes the Sixth Head and the Seventh Head was : that the former was *Laureated,* and the latter *Diademed*. The simple truth is, that, whether the Laurel or the Diadem was borne by the Emperor, it was borne, not as a *pontifical*, but as a *secular*, badge : and, as for the sacerdotal title of *Pontifex Maximus*, it was borne alike, *without any distinguishing addition,* by all the successive Emperors, from Augustus down to Gratian who resigned or rejected it. The very inscription, indeed, to Dioclesian, cited by the writer in evidence, affords no testimony at all. In it, the Emperor is addressed, not as *Diademato Pontifici Maximo*, but simply as *Pontifici Maximo :* and, as for Mr. Gibbon's very true statement that he first adopted the diadem, the writer forgets to tell us, that he adopted it from the eastern magnificence of Persia, not as a discriminative badge of the *Pontificate*, but as the ensign of *Royalty*.

It is urged, however, that power to practise forty-two months is given to the Seventh Head when revived as an Eighth Polity. Whence, that Eighth Polity can only be the Papacy.

Now, in reply, I beg to ask : WHERE is it ever said, that such power should be given to the revived Seventh Head ?

In making such an assertion, the writer must have neglected to examine the grammatical construction of the Greek original. The power is said to be given to IT in the neuter gender, as referring to the neuter substantive *Therion* or *Wild-Beast :* not given to IT in the feminine gender, which is necessary to produce a grammatical reference to the feminine substantive

Cephalè or *Head**. In short, the power is given
to the *Wild-Beast*. Under what particular *Head*
or *Heads* the Wild-Beast would exercise the given
power, the prophecy nowhere informs us.

On the whole, then, whether we respect Homogeneity or History or Grammar, the present
Scheme hopelessly breaks down : and, if it be
thought that I have considered it at too great
a length, my excuse must be its plausibility,
wherein it much excels its prototype and predecessor.

3. Thus, again, the prophetically declared *short-
lived* Seventh Head, has been actually and gravely
pronounced to be the *long-continuing* Carlovingian
Roman-Emperorship.

But a Polity, which, either in France or in
Germany, subsisted more than a thousand years,
cannot well be said to have *continued a short space :*
and, furthermore, when it fell in the year 1806,
it was not, as the prophecy requires, slain by the
sword of war, but simply ceased to exist by a
formal abdication.

---

* It may be useful to give the original Greek. Καὶ ἐδόθη
ΑΥΤΩΙ (scil. *θηρίῳ*) ἐξουσία ποιῆσαι μῆνας τεσσαράκοντα δύο.—
Rev. xiii. 5.

4. Yet, again, the Seventh Head has been, with pre-eminent confidence, recently declared to be the Line of the Western Roman Emperors from Honorius to the temporary extinction of the Latin Empire: while its revival is found in the inauguration of the Carlovingian Empire.

But this ill-digested Scheme fails in every particular.

It evinces a total ignorance of the very Principle of Roman Law, which, as appearing again and again in the records of History, and as fully established (if it needed any such additional establishment) by the Institutes of Justinian, always deemed the Roman Emperorship an UNIT by whatever number of Individuals it might be administered. Hence, instead of viewing the Western Emperorship of Honorius (by Mr. Mede denominated the *Demi-Cæsar*) as a distinct Head or Polity, the Principle of Roman Law identified it both with the Augustan Emperorship and with the Constantinian Emperorship and with the Carlovingian Emperorship.

Furthermore, it stands confuted by naked matter of fact, as compared with the requisitions of Prophecy.

The Roman Empire, after all its various changes,

during which, in the eye of Prophecy, it never loses its *identity*, is finally to go into destruction under its revived Seventh Head: and *that*, so terribly, and so perfectly, as to leave not a vestige of its multiplied polities behind. With its destruction, is to be associated that of the False Prophet: and the destined theatre of these great events is, again and again, marked out to be Palestine; while the immediate neighbourhood of Jerusalem and the Dead Sea is yet more definitely specified.

Now, we may confidently appeal to History, whether as the present Scheme plainly requires, any such facts marked the extinction of the Carlovingian-Roman Emperorship in the year 1806.

III. Directly opposed to these and the like untenable schemes, the view, which, by the mere compulsion of stubborn facts, I was led to adopt considerably more than thirty years ago (it was *propounded* in the year 1818), and which has since, by an additional palmary fact, received a full establishment, shrinks not, so far as I have been able to discover, from any severity of SIFTING: while, in corroboration of the evidence afforded by facts, it stands out imperiously required by the known Principle of Roman Law.

1. According to the force of that Law (which, in the Institutes of Justinian, is taken for granted, as if any formal proof of so well-known a matter were plainly a work of supererogation), the Emperorship of the Romans did not ultimately fall until the year 1806.

But, during the course of its long subsistence, no Seventh Head *could* spring up : for, in that case, we should have the anomaly of two distinct and different Supreme Heads reigning simultaneously and conjointly.

Yet the predicted and fully-described Seventh Head, be it what Power it might, *must* spring up very shortly *before* the fall of its predecessor : for, if it sprang up indefinitely *after* the fall, the Empire, during the interval between the fall of one Head and the rise of another, would for a season be left without a Head*.

* The prophecy recognises no such interval between Head and Head, as that one Head should have *completely* fallen *before* another was ready to take its place. Abeyances there were : but an abeyance is the very reverse of an extinction. When the Seventh Head is mortally wounded by the sword, all its predecessors having already fallen, the Empire, having now no living Head, is left in a state of political death or non-existence *as* an Empire. But the deadly wound is healed : and, by the revival of the sword-slain Seventh Head, not by the rise of any new Eighth Head, the defunct Empire is re-

3. The event exactly confirmed the necessary anticipation.

Until the year 1806, the Roman Emperorship did not fall. Therefore the Seventh Head *cannot* have appeared in the course of some distant age *remotely before* that year : but it *must* have appeared so *shortly before* it, as to be ready to take the place of the now sickening Roman Emperorship as soon as ever its increasing debility should terminate in its political death.

Such, accordingly, was the event.

The Roman Emperorship, gradually sickening and pining away by the secession or abstraction of its Feudatories, fell in the year 1806. But the destined short-lived and sword-slain and now at length revived Seventh Head had sprung up in the year 1804 : and was thus ready to take the place of the old Roman Emperorship and to perform *its* destined part in the great political drama.

IV. The series of the apocalyptic Vials, as connected with the Emperorship of the French, leaves

vived also. Now, in the whole course of the Roman Empire, under all its Seven Heads, there is no interval without a living Head, save that which occurs between the slaying and the revival of the same single Seventh Head. The whole of this political machinery is, in fact, borrowed from the fabled hydra of animal life.

no doubt, that the Fifth Vial has been poured out.

Hence, in the course of regular succession, the Effusion of the Sixth Vial may next in order be expected.

1. We have recently heard a warning stroke upon the prophetic bell : we may expect, therefore, from the disposition of the apocalyptic series, shortly to hear another.

I say *shortly :* because, on the Principle of Synchronisation which (as Mede well shows) is the very life-blood of apocalyptic interpretation, the Seventh Vial brings us to the close of the 1260 years.

Now, as I have already stated, there is much reason to believe that that famous period will expire in the year 1864.

Hence, if the Seventh Vial begins to flow in the year 1864, we may now, in the year 1853, be morally sure, that the Effusion of the Sixth Vial must needs occur *shortly*.

2. I once thought, that the Sixth Vial marked a Gradual Drying up of the mystic Euphrates : and, thence, as I could not but see the Gradual Declension of the Ottoman Power, I supposed it to be *even now* flowing.

But, in such an opinion, I was certainly mistaken.

The real question is : whether, in apocalyptic chronology, the Effusion of the Sixth Vial marks the *Commencement,* or the *Completion*, of the Drying up of the mystic Euphrates.

3. By the almost unanimous consent of commentators, the effect of the Sixth Trumpet, by loosing the Four Angels or Ottomanic Sultanies bound for a season in the region of the great river Euphrates, indicates the *Rise* of the Ottoman Power.

Hence, correspondingly and homogeneously, we may conclude, that the Drying up of that same river indicates the *Downfall* of that same Empire.

4. The principle of this harmonious interpretation of the Sixth Trumpet and the Sixth Vial is that of well-ascertained symbolisation.

A river, mentioned *generally* and without any particular *local restriction*, denotes a regularly politied nation.

Hence, when some *particular river* is specified by name, the nation, characterised by that river from the circumstance of the river being its chief or regal stream, is intended.

The Euphrates, therefore, being the principal river of Turkey and flowing through the midst of it, becomes the appropriate symbol of the Turkish Empire.

5. The same river had already, for the same reason, been employed by Isaiah to typify the Assyrian Empire.

Forasmuch as this people refuseth the waters of Shiloah that go softly, and rejoice in Rezin and Remaliah's son: now, therefore, behold, the Lord bringeth up upon them the waters of the river strong and many, the King of Assyria and all his glory. And he shall come up over all his channels, and go over all his banks.   And he shall pass through Judah: he shall overflow and go over: he shall reach even to the neck*.

Here, the overflowing of the Euphrates, always by way of excellence denominated simply *the River*, imports the victorious progress of Assyria under her King.

Conversely, therefore, when the River, still the Euphrates, is smitten into seven shallow streams so that men may go over it dryshod; and when this is done to make a way for Israel out of Assyria, whither he had been led captive: the

* Isaiah. viii. 6–8.

import must be the Dissolution of the Power *then* symbolised by the River.

The same remark applies to the Tongue of the Egyptian Sea or the Delta of the Nile. When this is utterly destroyed to open a passage for Judah from the West, such a management of the symbol will import the Destruction of the *then* Governing Power of Egypt*.

6. With Mr. Mede, I think, that the imagery of *the Drying up the Euphrates* upon the Effusion of the Sixth Vial has been borrowed from *the Smiting of the Euphrates into seven streams* in the prophecy of Isaiah.

But I am willing to go yet farther. I not only admit a mutuation of imagery: I likewise incline to deem the *Smiting of the Euphrates* and the *Drying up of the Euphrates,* to bear precisely *the same meaning,* and to be strictly *one and the same event.*

In each case, we may observe, that the Euphrates has *not* a way opened through the *midst* of it, the waters in their full force standing like a wall above and below, as when Israel passed through the western horn of the Red Sea and again through the stream of the river Jordan.

* Isaiah. xi. 11–16 ; xxvii. 12, 13.

On the contrary, the waters are absolutely *dried up*: and thus the great River is made so shallow, as to present no obstacle to those who would pass, not *through* it, but *over* it.

This is a distinction, which must be carefully borne in mind: for the two cases are essentially different.

A way may be miraculously opened *through* a river, by dividing its stream: while the river itself is in full force and the very reverse of being dried up.

And a way may be miraculously prepared *over the bed* of a river, by a complete drying up of the river itself: while, in that case, there is no division of its stream so as to form a passage.

The distinction before us is of prime importance: because, unless I greatly mistake, it effectually demonstrates, that the Euphrates, when described as either *dried up* or as *smitten into shallow runlets*, cannot be the *literal*, but must be the *symbolical*, Euphrates. Of course, I deny not the possibility of a miracle which should either totally dry up the Euphrates or convert it into a number of shallow brooks. Yet, when, on the supposition that the *literal* Euphrates is meant, a way might just as effectually be pre-

pared for the returning Israelites by a *division* of
the stream so as to afford a passage between its
suspended waters : and when we recollect, that
God never works superfluously : it does not seem
probable, that the *whole* of such a river should be
needlessly dried up ; which yet we must believe, if
we suppose the *literal* Euphrates to be meant.

7. In Isaiah, the purpose, for which the
Euphrates is made shallow and the Delta of the
Nile destroyed, is to afford a highway, for Israel
from Assyria, and for Judah from the West
especially, though without *an exclusion* of the *four
corners of the earth.*

The indication of this purpose distinctly marks
the chronology of the prophecy.

We know from Daniel, that the dispersion of
the holy people will be finished, and that his
nation will be delivered at the close of the Three
Times and a Half : and, from Isaiah, we learn,
that the restoration of Israel will synchronise with
the restoration of Judah, and will, therefore, occur
at the close of the same grand period*. Hence
it follows, that the smiting of the Euphrates into
seven shallow streams, and the synchronical destruction of the Tongue or Delta of the Egyptian

* Dan. xii. 1, 6, 7 : Isaiah. xi. 11–16 ; xxvii. 12, 13.

Sea, each occurring to prepare a way for the two grand divisions of God's ancient people, must obviously occur some short time *before* the expiration of the Three Times and a Half*.

8. This, at once, brings out another synchronism.

The apocalyptic Drying up of the Euphrates stands precisely in the same chronological position as the Smiting of the Euphrates into seven shallow streams announced by Isaiah.

Hence we may be morally certain, that the same event, be it literal or be it figurative, is set forth in each prophecy alike.

But I should almost venture to say, that the very necessity of the case, in each prophecy alike, requires us to adopt a figurative interpretation.

Hence, the Drying up of the Euphrates or the Smiting it into seven shallow streams will denote, not any such *literal* infliction upon the *literal* river, but the Downfall of the Empire symbolised by the river at the period to which the two allied prophecies refer : that is to say, it will note the Completed Downfall of the Ottoman Empire.

9. This conclusion forthwith determines the

* Nothing can be more correct than the bestowing upon the Nile the name of the Egyptian Sea. It was of old denominated *Oceames*, or the *Ocean*.

c

character of the apocalyptic Kings from the East.

The Smiting of the Euphrates into seven shallow streams prepares a highway for the Ten Tribes of Israel out of Assyria, whither their forefathers had been deported.

The Drying up of the Euphrates, similarly and at the very same time, prepares the way of the Kings from the rising of the sun.

Therefore, most plainly, the Kings from the rising of the sun can be no other than the Ten Tribes of Israel.

10. Furthermore: since the infliction upon the Euphrates must thus be interpreted figuratively, as denoting, not any exsiccation of the literal river, but the Downfall of the Empire symbolised by it: homogeneity requires, that the Destruction of the Delta of the Nile or of the Egyptian Sea, which is foretold conjointly in the same prophecy, should be similarly interpreted.

Hence, as the Downfall of the Ottoman Power is foretold under the image of the Exsiccation of the Euphrates: so the Downfall of the Power paramount in Egypt is similarly foretold by the Destruction of the Nile.

In each case, an impediment is to be removed,

and a way is to be prepared for the return of the whole House of Israel, both from the East and from the West.

Isaiah, after mentioning the various regions out of which they are to be restored, emphatically sums up the whole by the striking declaration : *The Lord shall set up an ensign for the nations, and shall assemble the outcasts of Israel, and gather together the dispersed of Judah from the four corners of the earth**.

11. Thus, from the sufficiently obvious tenor of two connected prophecies, the imagery of the later prophecy (as Mede justly observes) being borrowed from the imagery of the earlier prophecy, we gather, that, at the effusion of the Sixth Vial,

---

* Isaiah. xi. 12. Perhaps it may be thought that the last clause in the chapter, *like as it was to Israel in the day that he came up out of the land of Egypt,* would import a literal passage through the Euphrates and the Nile : but it respects the *circumstance,* not the *mode,* of the exodus. This is clear from the total difference between the two *modes :* a difference so great as to preclude any just comparison. The Israelites, when they left Egypt, passed between the *divided* waters of the Red Sea and the river Jordan.   In neither case were those waters *dried up :* so far from it, indeed, that Jordan, as we are expressly told, was then *overflowing all his banks.* But, in the still future return of the Israelites and the Jews, the waters of the Euphrates will be *dried up*, and the Delta of the Nile will be *destroyed.*

the Drying up of the mystic Euphrates does not *commence*, but is *completed*: in other words, the oracle of the Sixth Vial announces, not the *Gradual Decay* of the Turkish Empire, but its *Completed Downfall*.

12. I once thought differently: but, as in conscience bound, I freely acknowledge myself to have been on *that* point mistaken.

In truth, the *early* commencement of decay in the Ottoman Power perfectly agrees with, and thus corroborates, the deduction which has already been drawn. If the effusion of the Sixth Vial be judged to mark the *Commencement* of the decay of Turkey, the whole arrangement of the series of Vials will be dislocated.

The decay commenced almost immediately after the fatal defeat at Zenta, in the year 1697, where I place the passing away of the Second Great Woe*. From the time of that defeat, the Ottoman Power has experienced a gradual and regular declension. It may not be uninteresting, as it certainly is not unimportant, to mark the several steps in its decay.

The Treaty of Carlowicz, in the year 1699, deprived the Sultan of all sway in Hungary and

* See my Sacred Calendar of Prophecy. book iv. ch. 7. § ii.

Transylvania, leaving to him only the town of Temeswar : and, furthermore, it despoiled him of Azof, and the Ucraine, and Podolia, and Dalmatia.

In the year 1718, the treaty of Passarowitz drove the Turks from Temeswar, and destroyed all hope of recovering their power in Dalmatia and Hungary.

In the year 1771, the Crimea was taken from Turkey.

In the year 1774, the treaty of Kainardge secured the independence of the Tartars of the Crimea and Bessarabia and the Kouban.

By a treaty signed at Constantinople in the year 1784, the Ottoman Sovereignty, even in its shadow, totally disappeared throughout those provinces.

The treaty of Bucharest, in the year 1812, gave to Russia all the fortified places on the left bank of the Danube between Galatz and the Black Sea.

In the year 1816, Servia detached itself from the Turkish Empire : and, on the condition of paying an annual tribute, secured its real independence under a nominal Suzerainty.

In the year 1821, the Greek Insurrection commenced with the capture of Patras : and, subsequently, an independent Greek kingdom, having Athens for its capital, has been established.

In the year 1829, the treaty of Adrianople proclaimed the independence of Moldavia and Servia and Wallachia : for, in those regions, the Ottoman Authority is now only nominal.

In the year 1830, the Sultan was deprived of the Suzerainty of Algeria, which henceforward became a French Province.

And, in the year 1840, Russia, Prussia, Austria, and England, guaranteed Egypt to Mehemet Ali and his family, on the sole condition of paying a tribute to the Sultan*.

Such a course of regular decay has been rarely witnessed†. But, if we suppose the Effusion of

---

* For these dates, I am indebted to a pamphlet by M. Pougoulat, entitled *La France et la Russie à Constantinople*.

† It is a remarkable circumstance, that, concurrently with the *political* drying up of the figurative waters of the mystic Euphrates, there should also be simultaneously going on a *physical* drying up of them by the process of a gradual depopulation.

For the knowledge of this striking fact, I am indebted, through my friend Mr. Harcourt, to Colonel Rose.

That gentleman, having been our Consul-general in Syria, and afterward the Chargé d'Affaires at Constantinople, had ample opportunity of becoming intimately acquainted with the character of the Turkish Population and Power. He is of opinion, that the practice of polygamy inevitably produces a

the Sixth Vial to mark the *Commencement* of such
decay and not its *Completion,* we shall find our-

numerical wasting away of the people : and the result is, not
merely a theoretical necessity, but a veritable fact. The
Turkish Population is drying up by a rapid diminution of its
numbers : and, as Mr. Harcourt observes, this weakening of
their Power, after it has reached a certain point, would be a
natural preparation for the return of the Jews.

This two-fold wasting away of Turkey, *political* and *physical*,
is very important under yet another aspect.

By its exact and minute accomplishment of the prophecy of
the Drying up of the Euphrates, it proves the correctness of
the application of that prophecy to Turkey : while such an
application of it was itself *anteriorly* required by the very
necessity of the demonstrated Principle of Symbolisation. As,
in accordance with this Principle, the Euphrates was employed
by Isaiah to typify the Assyrian Empire : so, analogously, on
the same Principle, St. John employs it to typify the Ottoman
Empire, which now stands geographically in the place of the
old Assyrian Empire.

I have understood, that the Turks themselves have long
been impressed with a belief, that their Empire is destined to
be subverted by Russia : and the aspirations of Russia, at least
since the days of the Empress Catharine, are abundantly evident. In all human probability, they will be accomplished :
but we have no prophetic ground for specifying the *precise*
year of the Downfall of the Ottoman Power. Should the Czar,
through such a conquest, become Lord of Syria, he will, by
virtue of that acquisition, also become that King of the North,
who, in Daniel's prophecy, plays so conspicuous a part at the
Time of the End, or at the close of the 1260 years.—Dan. xi.
40. Truly, we live in a period so pregnant with extraordinary
events, that we may well be stirred up to no ordinary degree of
seriousness.

selves compelled to place that Effusion in the year 1699: an arrangement, which is plainly intolerable.

V. The Turkish Empire has not yet fallen: therefore the Sixth Vial cannot as yet have been poured out.

1. There is a matter immediately connected with it, which I must take this opportunity of noticing: and I do it all the rather, because it has led to a good deal of expositorial inaccuracy.

The three unclean spirits like frogs have very commonly been thought to issue respectively, from the mouths of the Dragon and the Wild-Beast and the False Prophet, *as soon* as the Sixth Vial begins to flow. Hence it is assumed, as a matter of course, that, upon the Effusion of the Sixth Vial, St. John *beheld* them issue from the three specified mouths.

But nothing of the kind is said in the prophecy.

St. John beheld them, not *in the act of issuing*, but *after they had issued*.

What the Apostle describes himself to have *seen* is the going forth of the three spirits to gather together the Kings of the whole Roman World to the war of the Great Day of God

Almighty; not their act of issuing from the three specified mouths.

The passage runs thus.

I saw, from the mouth of the Dragon and from the mouth of the Wild-Beast and from the mouth of the False Prophet, three unclean spirits as frogs.

It is subjoined, *which had come forth.* This makes the sense of the passage somewhat more explicit: but it is not necessary: and Griesbach rejects the past participle, which more fully brings out the sense*. Still the sense remains the same. When the Sixth Vial was poured out, the Apostle beheld, stationed upon the Roman Platform, three unclean spirits as frogs, which had *already* issued from the three mouths of the Dragon and the Wild-Beast and the False Prophet: and then he *saw* them immediately go forth with the object of forming a mighty Confederacy of the Papal Kings. The formation of the Confederacy is the immediate consequence of the Completed Exhaustion of the Waters of the mystic Euphrates; or, in other words, it is the immediate result of the Downfall of the Ottoman Power produced by the Effusion of the Sixth Vial.

* Gr. ἐκπορευθέντα.

2. From the matters now before us, we may reasonably anticipate, that the Destruction of Turkey will produce the outbreak of that fearful war, which, commencing in Europe, will, at the Time of the End or at the Close of the 1260 years, ✗ pass into Palestine and Egypt and the East.

Then, as Daniel speaks, will there be *a time of trouble such as never was since there was a nation*: and then Michael, the Great Prince, will stand up for the children of the Prophet's people; and that ancient people, whether Jews or Israelites, will be delivered out of the hand of their enemies.

3. The agents, who stir up this war, will be the three unclean spirits.

✗ As they do not issue from the mouths of the Dragon and the Wild-Beast and the False Prophet *immediately* upon the pouring of the Sixth Vial, but were beheld by St. John as having *already* thus issued, we may reasonably suppose them to be even now in existence, though they have not as yet formally gone forth to the Kings of the Earth to gather them to the battle of that great day of God Almighty.

This will not occur, until the Sixth Vial shall have been poured out and until the Ottoman Power shall have been overturned.

✗ supposed to be _1866_

Meanwhile, supposing them to be even now in existence, and judging of their characters from their parentage, we may easily form no improbable conjecture as to what they are. At any rate, purely as a fact, we may now perceive, ready prepared and harmoniously co-operating for a bad end, Infidelity, and Military Despotism called into action by Anarchy, and Jesuitism of the most arrogant and tyrannical Ultramontane School.

To assure any such co-operation might once have been thought paradoxical: but we have already seen enough of their conjoined practices to feel little difficulty in believing, that they will cordially act together against pure religion, and that they will be the main artificers of the final great Anti-christian Confederation.

VI. In the present day, with so many signs of the times pressing upon us, we cannot wonder, that the long lost, or at least long overlooked, Ten Tribes of Israel, should have recently called up no small amount of interest and attention. Hence, we are in a manner constrained to inquire, whether, in the remarkable crisis at which we have arrived, there is any reasonable prospect of their discovery.

1. Dr. Buchanan thinks, that, in various de-

tachments, they exist through nearly the whole of Asia.

2. Dr. Grant of Utica, in the United States of America, is confident that he has found them, partly converted to Christianity from a very early period, and partly still unconverted, in the mountainous region which coincides with the ancient Assyria Proper, and which the Greeks called *Adiabenè*.

3. The missionary, Mr. Samuel, is persuaded, that he has found the first deported Two Tribes and a Half in the rugged country of Daghistan, which stretches for a hundred and forty miles along the western shore of the Caspian Sea.

4. And, lastly, a valuable layman, Sir George Rose, in a small work written in a beautiful spirit of Christian piety, has lately revived an opinion, first, I believe, advanced in the year 1784, that the Ten Tribes will be found in the Afghans.

I much incline to think, that, in all these opinions, there is a measure of truth : though some of them might have been propounded more correctly, because less exclusively.

VII. The country, to which the Ten Tribes were deported, is very definitely marked out in Scripture.

1. Pul and Tiglath-Pileser first carried away the transjordanic Israelites; Reuben, and Gad, and the Half Tribe of Manasseh : and, next, about nineteen years later, Shalmaneser carried away the remaining Seven Tribes and a Half of the cisjordanic Israelites.

The whole Ten Tribes, however, were removed into the same region of Assyria Proper and into parts of the adjoining border country of Media. For they are alike said to have been carried into Assyria and into the cities of the Medes : that is to say, with a more specific geographical designation, into Halah, and unto Habor the river of Gozan, and into the mountain districts of the Assyrian Empire, Hara or Haran*.

Thus the region, into which the entire Ten Tribes were carried, was that, which the Greeks mainly called *Adiabenè*, and which is specially identified by its having a river that still bears the name of *Habor*.† It lies north-east of Nineveh, south-east of Lake Van, and directly west of

---

* See 2 Kings. xv. 29; xvii. 3, 6, 18 : 1 Chron. v. 26.

† Εἰ μὴ τις ὑπὲρ Εὐφράτην ἐκτείνει τὰς ἐλπίδας, καὶ τοὺς ἐκ τῆς Ἀδιαβηνῆς ὁμοφύλους οἴεται προσαμύνειν· οἱ δὲ, οὔτε δι' αἰτίαν ἄλογον τηλικούτῳ πολέμῳ συμπλέξουσιν ἑαυτοὺς, οὔτε βουλευσαμένοις κακῶς ὁ Πάρθος ἐπιτρέψει.—Joseph. de Bell. Judaic. lib. ii. c. 16. § 4, p. 1089. Edit. Hudson. The river *Habor*, flowing through a

the Lake of Ooroomiah: and it coincides with
the original *Assyria Proper*, as contradistinguished from the much more widely-extended
Assyrian Empire.

2. It may seem extraordinary, that the region,
described more particularly as the land of Gozan
and Haran, should have been vacant, and thence
should have been ready to receive such a body of
emigrants as the Ten Tribes. But this circumstance is readily accounted for by the boast of
Sennacherib, which purports, that his fathers and
predecessors had exterminated the prior inhabitants of that district, annoyed probably by their
marauding incursions into the lower provinces of
the Empire: a matter of no easy accomplishment,
when both the character of the free-booters and
the mountainous nature of the country are considered; and thence giving occasion to much vain-
glorious boasting*. The districts of Ashur or

land of *Zozans* or *Gozans*, exactly as it is described in 2 Kings.
xvii. 6, falls into the Tigris north of Mosul. See Laurie's
Dr. Grant and the Mountain Nestorians, p. 115, et passim.
Mr. Layard writes the name of the river, *Khabour:* and states,
that its junction with the Tigris takes place at Dereboun.—
Discoveries in Nineveh, p. 51. The letter Cheth has the force
of either the simple H or the compound CH. Hence, *Habor*
and *Khabour* are the same appellation.

* See 2 Kings. xix. 12 ; Isaiah. xxxvii. 11, 12.

Assyria Proper, which geographically compre-
hended the country of Adiabenè, the policy of the
three Assyrian Monarchs led them to people afresh
with the deported Israelites : for, in these, broken
by conquest and far removed from their own
country, they naturally expected to find more
quiet and less troublesome neighbours than the
expelled previous occupants*.

3. Who these previous occupants were, it is
not very difficult to determine.

They were plainly, I think, a remnant of those
military children of Cush, who, when their great
leader Nimrod was divinely compelled to leave
Babylon, went forth with him into the land
originally occupied by Ashur; and, in the lower
part of the country, on the banks of the Tigris,
founded Nineveh†. Meanwhile, the mountain
districts were tenanted by turbulent bodies of

* Mr. Layard mentions, that, near the head-waters of the
Euphrates, as is learned from the bull inscriptions, Sennacherib waged one of his most important wars.—*Discoveries in
the Ruins of Nineveh*, p. 342.

† See Gen. x. 10–12. Mr. Layard's discoveries, and the
tradition of the country which makes Ashur, in the Chaldee
form Athur, the lieutenant of Nimrod, fully establish the mar-
ginal rendering in our Bible Translation : *Out of that land*
(Babel), *he* (Nimrod) *went forth into Assyria and builded
Nineveh.*

haughty Cuthites, mingled with fragments of the original Ashurites: and these were the people, whose extermination by the later Assyrian kings made room for the subdued and expatriated Israelites.

4. It is not a little remarkable, that the parallel expulsion of a branch of the same warlike people from Egypt should have made room for the ancestors of the Israelites in the days of Jacob and Joseph.

The expulsion itself is not mentioned in Scripture: but, clearly, the Israelites could not have been placed in the fertile land of Goshen, unless that land had then been empty; and we learn from other sources, that the Hycsos or Pallic Shepherd-Kings, after their first invasion of Egypt, had actually been driven out very shortly before the descent of the Israelites under Jacob*.

These warlike shepherds, like their kindred the Philistines and the Phœnicians, were of the great military House of Cush: and their character of Palli or Shepherds, which implied anything rather than a poetically love-making and pastorally-piping race, is impressed alike upon the exterminated

---

* For a full discussion of this curious subject, see my Origin of Pagan Idolatry. book vi. chap. 5.

Cuthim of Adiabenè and the expelled Cuthim of Egypt.   Each country had its Goshen or Gozan : and, as the *Gozan* of Adiabenè, now slightly corrupted into *Zozan,* denotes, we are informed, *Pasture ;* so the *Goshen* of Egypt, a name affixed by its invaders from the shores of the Persian Gulf, similarly denotes *The Land of Pasturage* or *The Land of Shepherds*.*

Well might Sennacherib boast of the prowess of his fathers in exterminating such a race from such a country : for, in whatever quarter of the globe they appeared, they were always the most warlike of the sons of men, and in each successive great Empire always had the preëminence.

VIII. Here, then, in a most accurately specified region ; that, to wit, where the western boundary of Media touches the eastern or north-eastern boundary of Assyria Proper : the expatriated Ten Tribes were *originally* planted, whatever colonies or offshoots might *subsequently* penetrate into other parts of Asia.

Accordingly, down to the fifth century of the Christian era, we have distinct evidence, that *there* (at least as the nucleus of the Ten Tribes)

* The word *Goshen,* as well as the kindred word *Palli* (whence *Palestine* or *Pallisthan*), is, I believe, Sanscrit.

D

they were, and that *there* they continued to dwell.

1. Josephus attests, that Ezra, full five centuries before Christ, or about two hundred years after their completed deportation by Shalmaneser, not only read to the proper Jews at Babylon the letter of Xerxes or Artaxerxes, but likewise sent a copy of it into Media to their brethren the Israelites: and he adds, that, while (with the exception of many detached individuals, who journeyed with their effects to Babylon, wishing to return to Jerusalem) Two Tribes only went back to Palestine and became subject to the Romans; the whole multitude of the Israelites, to the amount of innumerable myriads, remained behind, down even to his own day, in the region beyond the Euphrates, whither they had been originally carried away*.

2. From another statement of the Jewish Historian, it seems to have been in his time familiarly known, that the Israelites were yet dwelling in the same land of Adiabenè beyond the Euphrates, whither they had been successively transported by Pul and Tiglath-Pileser and Shalmaneser. For he represents Agrippa, in the speech by which he

* Joseph. Ant. Judaic. lib. xi. c. 5. § 2. p. 482.

would dissuade the Jews from entering into that fatal war with the Romans which issued in the destruction of their city and temple, as urging, among other matters, that they must not vainly look for aid from their brethren in Adiabenè beyond the Euphrates : inasmuch as, even if they had the power, they would not lightly embark in such an undertaking ; but, in truth, that it was not in their power, for the dominance of the Parthians, whose Empire lay between them and Jerusalem, would not suffer it*.

3. So again, Jerome, at the beginning of the fifth century, attests, even repeatedly, as a matter then incapable of contradiction : that the Ten Tribes still remained in the land of their original deportation, having never, *collectively* or *universally*, departed from it, whatever *colonies* or *insulated detachments* might have gone forth†.

4. I may add, that oblique notices of the same circumstance appear in more than one place of Holy Scripture itself.

* Joseph. de Bell. Judaic. lib. ii. c. 16. § 4. p. 1089. I have already quoted this passage, as marking the country of the deportation.

† Hieron. Comment. in Hier. xxxi. 16. Comment. in Ezek. xvi. 55 ; xxiii. 1 ; xxxvii. 15. Oper. tom. iv. p. 298, 378–379, 399, 447.

When the Apostles first exercised the miraculous gift of tongues, it is said, that, among the foreign brethren out of every nation under heaven then dwelling at Jerusalem, there were *Parthians and Medes :* that is to say, strangers out of the very region into which the Ten Tribes had been deported*.

In like manner, St. Paul, when pleading his cause before Agrippa, speaks familiarly, as if it were a matter well known, of *the Twelve Tribes* (the Ten Tribes as well as the Two Tribes) *hoping to come to the promise made of God unto their fathers†.*

St. James, likewise, addresses his Epistle to *the Twelve Tribes,* which are described by him as *scattered abroad‡.*   I consider this to be a very remarkable attestation : for it not only shows, that the Twelve Tribes, whether viewed as the Two Tribes or the Ten Tribes, were not then confined within the limits of a single district ; but, from the whole context, it additionally shows, that members of *all* the Twelve Tribes, that *Dodecaphylon* specified by St. Paul, had, even at that early time, embraced Christianity.

5. It is a matter of uncertainty, when the

* Acts. ii. 5–9.   † Acts. xxvi. 6, 7.   ‡ James. i. 1, 2.

apocryphal Esdras lived. Some place him before, and some after, the time of our Lord. Internal evidence seems to prove, that the Work, which bears his name, was the production of a Rabbinical Jew. This, however, is a matter of no great consequence to my present purpose. His Work contains a very curious attestation, though considerably mixed with fable, to the fully existing persuasion, that the Ten Tribes had been carried beyond the Euphrates to the precise country marked out for them in Scripture History.

Those, says he, *are the Ten Tribes, which were carried away prisoners out of their own land in the time of Osea the King, whom Salmanasar the King of Assyria led away captive. And he carried them over the waters : and so they came into another land. But they took this counsel among themselves : that they would leave the multitude of the heathen, and go forth into a further country where never mankind dwelt, that they might there keep their statutes which they never kept in their own land. And they entered into Euphrates by the narrow passages of the river : for the Most High then showed signs for them, and held still the flood till they were passed over. For, through that country, there was a great way to go, namely, of a year and a half : and the same region is called* ARSARETH. *Then dwelt they there until the latter time : and now, when they shall begin to come, the Highest shall stay the springs of the stream again, that they may go through*.*

There is a singular mixture of truth and romance in this statement. Yet, with proper discrimination, I cannot but consider it as valuable.

It correctly informs us, that they entered into Euphrates by *the narrow passages* of the river, and not lower down where the stream would be so broad as to offer a serious impediment : and, when they return, he speaks of their crossing *near the springs of the stream* again. But he gratuitously adds, in each case, a miraculous interposition, which, after the manner of the passage through the Red Sea and Jordan, should hold still the flood till they were passed over.

This idea, in connexion with the Euphrates, seems to have been borrowed from the text in Isaiah, where it is said that the River, as the Euphrates was called by way of eminence, should be smitten into seven shallow streams, so that those, who were returning from Assyria, namely the Ten Tribes, might be enabled to go over dry-

* 2 Esdr. xiii. 40–47.

shod : while it is added, *like as it was to Israel in the day that he came up out of the land of Egypt**.

But, if the idea of the apocryphal writer thus originated, he did not observe, that the comparison at the close of the text respects, not the *mode,* but the *circumstance,* of the exode : for, in the prophecy, the flood is not *held still* as were the waters of Jordan, but is so *exhausted* by being divided into shallow runlets, that men might pass over without wetting their feet.

Furthermore : this same Rabbinical writer speaks of their passing into a country beyond the Euphrates, which, as would obviously be the case when a whole people moved with their flocks and herds, occasioned them a long and tedious journey : and that country he describes as one *where never mankind dwelt.*

Here he is accurate, so far as the *character* of the country is concerned ; for the Israelites found it empty by reason of the extermination, or at least the removal, of the former inhabitants : but he is inaccurate, though the origination of his inaccuracy is easily detected, when he says that *mankind never dwelt there.*

Again : he is sufficiently correct in saying, that

* Isaiah. xi. 15, 16.

the Ten Tribes, separated from the multitude of
the heathen, wished henceforth to keep their
statutes, which they never kept in their own land:
for, even to this day, they seem, by frequent
intercourse with each other (as Dr. Buchanan
states), to have continued tolerably clear of apostasy ; and, when the false Esdras wrote, they seem
(as we gather from Josephus) to have still carefully retained their national statutes.

Finally, unless I greatly mistake, we have a
direct verbal intimation given us by Esdras, that
the country, which they would reach by crossing
at the narrow passages of the Euphrates, is the
very country, to which Scripture History directs
us. The region, where they settled, was called,
he tells us, ARSARETH. It seems tolerably evident,
that, by the slight corruption of inserting a single
letter, ARSARETH is no other than ARARETH : for
so, both the mountain of the Ark's appulse, and
the land of Armenia in its widest extent, were
equally denominated*. It was plainly in close
connexion with the great Assyrian Empire : for,
to Ararat or Armenia, Adrammelech and Sharezer,
the sons of Sennacherib king of Assyria, fled,
after the murder of their father, as he was wor-

* Gen. viii. 4 ; Isaiah. xxxvii. 38 ; Jerem. li. 27.

shipping in the house of his vulture-idol Nisroch at Nineveh. Probably, they were well aware, that they would be received and concealed by the Israelites of the Ten Tribes, who could entertain no very cordial affection for a King of Assyria.

IX. We seem to have now ascertained some very important particulars.

1. The Ten Tribes were deported into that mountainous region, which constituted Assyria Proper, which mainly coincided with the district by the Greeks called *Adiabenè*, and which bordered upon Media and Armenia.

2. In the early part of the fifth century, they were known to be still in this same region: though, doubtless, as, from the time of Shalmaneser downward, their numbers had continued to increase, *offshoots* or *colonies* would, in the true Oriental nomadic fashion, seek new settlements in various parts of Asia.

3. Finally, when St. James wrote his Epistle, about the year 60, some individual members of the Ten Tribes had already, in their scattered state, received the Gospel, though without losing their distinctive national character.

4. Now it certainly seems, that these particulars

afford a reasonable clue to the discovery of the long-lost Ten Tribes.

In point of FACT, we *know*, that they were, in the first instance, deported into Assyria : and the special part of Assyria is easily ascertainéd, by its being conterminous to the Western boundary of Media, in certain cities of which some of them are said to have been placed.

In point of PROPHECY, we are assured, that they will be restored *out of Assyria :* while, synchronically, the Dispersed of Judah will be gathered *out of the four corners of the earth.* But, though Assyria is thus specially mentioned as containing the nucleus of the Ten Tribes, we seem to gather, from the terms of the prediction, that they will also return, in various detachments, from other parts of Asia: such as, the Oriental Cush or Cusha-dwip within, as the Hindoos call the immense region of (what the Greeks called) the Asiatic Ethiopia ; and Elam, or some parts of Persia ; and Shinar, or the Babylonian Chaldea*.

5. From these matters, the conclusion is quite obvious.

* Isaiah. xi. 11–16 ; xxvii. 12, 13 : Hosea. xi. 8–11 : Zech. x. 6–11.

If the nucleus of the Ten Tribes, however diminished by colonising or by the hostile aggression of barbarous neighbours, is to be restored *out* of Assyria, they must, in order to the accomplishment of the prophecy, be still *in* Assyria.

X. Thus, so far as evidence, historical and scriptural, is concerned, the question stood, when Dr. Grant of Utica, in the United States of America, visited and spent some considerable time in the district, whither, it is well known, the Ten Tribes were originally carried.

His statement is: that he found matters precisely such as might have been expected from the knowledge which we already possessed.

1. The people were divided into two portions, distinct from each other and yet acknowledging the relationship of a common origin.

Part, from a very remote period, had been Christians : who received the name of *Nestorians*, because, with Nestorius, they would not apply to the Virgin Mary what they esteemed the unscriptural title of *Theotocos* or *Mother of God;* deeming it a virtual denial of Christ's humanity and thence a nullification of the doctrine of the atonement.

And Part still adhered exclusively to the Law

of Moses and the Levitical Ordinances : remaining, so far as Christianity was concerned, in an unconverted state.

We have only, says Dr. Grant, *to see the Jews and Nestorians together, and hear their mutual recriminations ; the one charging the other with apostasy from their ancient religion, and the latter accusing the former as the guilty rejecters of the Messiah : and we shall be at no loss how to account for the existing antipathy between the Nestorians and the Jews. I was recently present at just such an interview between them : and it required all the address I was master of to pacify and make them treat each other somewhat like brethren. When this was effected, they conversed freely together (though with occasional aspersion) on the subject of their former fraternal relation as* SONS OF ISRAEL : *a relation, so fully recognised by both parties, as to form the basis of their most pointed remarks*[*].

In this passage and elsewhere, Dr. Grant occasionally says *Jews* where he ought to have said *Israelites*. This very curious Work is entitled *The Nestorians, or the Lost Tribes :* and it contains much more to the same effect.

[*] The Nestorians. p. 201, 202.

We are certainly, said they, BENI ISRAEL : *there is no doubt of it*.*

Dr. Grant subjoins : *It is not a complicated history, requiring a detail of incidents or language liable to be misapprehended or forgotten. It is one simple bare fact, so unique and prominent in its character that there is no room for mistake. At the same time, the people are so peculiar in their language, character, and circumstances, that it was doubtless true of the whole, if of any. It is the one simple fact : that the Nestorians are, what they profess to be,* THE CHILDREN OF ISRAEL.

He then adds : *Direct and positive as is the testimony of the Nestorians themselves respecting their Hebrew ancestry, we need not rest so important a question on their testimony alone.—The Jews, who dwell among them, acknowledge the relationship. They admit, that the Nestorians are as truly the descendants of the Israelites as themselves.— Providentially for our cause, The Ten Tribes are not all nominally christian. A remnant seems to have been left as witnesses in the case. Dispersed through the country of the Nestorians, and surrounding them on every side, are some thousands of nominal Jews,*

* The Nestorians. p. 122.

still adhering to Judaism, who claim to be a part of the Ten Tribes carried away captive by the Kings of Assyria.—They testify, though sometimes reluctantly, that they and the Nestorians are brethren of the same stock; that they and the Nestorians have a common relation to the House of Israel, a common origin.—They are ashamed to admit, that such an apostasy has taken place from the faith of their fathers: and they are reluctant to acknowledge their worst enemies as brethren.—It is only to those who have gained their confidence, that they readily make the acknowledgment.—The first time I myself heard this testimony given by the Jews was March 6, 1840: which I recorded at the time as follows:

I received a visit from two learned Jews, Ezekiel and Daniel, of Ooroomiah: who, in presence of the Bishops Mar Yoosuph and Mar Eliyah, two Priests, and other Nestorians, most explicitly acknowledged, that the Nestorians were THE SONS OF ISRAEL; *a circumstance, with which, they affirmed, the Jews were well acquainted. Priest Dunka, for my sake, then asked them, if they were sure of the fact. They replied emphatically: that they knew, that the Nestorians were* CHILDREN OF ISRAEL; *but, as the Nestorians had departed from*

*the faith of their fathers, their people were ashamed
to own them as brethren.*

*More recently, other Jews have repeatedly made
the same statement to the writer and to some of
his associates in the mission. On one occasion,
their chief Rabbi confirmed the testimony of the
Hebrew origin of the Nestorians, while in their
synagogue, and in hearing of Messrs. Holliday,
Stocking, and myself. He said: that the Nestorians apostatised from the Jewish Faith in the
days of Christ or his Apostles.*

2. Dr. Grant mentions two particulars, which
must by no means be pretermitted.

Like the early Hebrew Church, the Nestorians
largely unite the *Observance of the Law* with *Belief in Christ.*

And, furthermore, in the midst of tribes of a
different tongue, they speak a modern dialect of
the Syriac, which differs not more from the ancient
Syriac, familiar as that dialect must have been to
the Ten Tribes from their neighbourhood to and
close connexion with the kingdom of Syria, than
modern Greek differs from ancient Greek.

XI. Sir George Rose, in a very ingenious
pamphlet which he has entitled *The Afghans
the Ten Tribes,* states: that Dr. Grant's opinion

has been impugned, and, as he thinks, over-thrown, by Dr. Robinson.

I have not seen the Work of that gentleman : and, therefore, can give no opinion as to the cogency of his arguments.

1. Sir George thinks it unnecessary to produce against Dr. Grant *all the erudition and acuteness* of Dr. Robinson, because he deems three main considerations sufficient to overthrow the system which he has raised.

(1.) He broadly contends, that the mere fact of the Nestorians having embraced Christianity many centuries ago completely negatives the theory, that they are descended from the deported Ten Tribes of Israel.

(2.) He thinks, that the supersession of Circum-cision by Baptism among them is equally fatal to the theory : and the ground, which he here takes, is, that, *For the Israelites to abandon Circumcision would be to renounce their share in the land of Canaan.*

(3.) And he argues : that the Assyrian Monarch would hardly have planted an indomitable nation like the Israelites in so difficult a country as the mountainous region now called *Curdistan*, when the rich and populous province of Media would have been so much better calculated for the king's political object*.

2. Whether Dr. Grant be right or wrong in his opinion, I certainly do not see that these arguments amount to a confutation.

(1.) Since, from the exordium of the Epistle of St. James, we learn, that various members of the Twelve Tribes, the *Ten* Tribes as well as the *Two*, described as *scattered abroad*, had, even in his time, embraced Christianity : it is difficult to comprehend, how that same profession of Christianity is, in the present day, incompatible with an Israelitish Descent.

(2.) Except Joshua and Caleb, all the circumcised Israelites, who left Egypt, had died in the wilderness : and none of those, who were subsequently born, had received the rite of Circumcision. Hence, according to the statement of Sir George Rose, they must all have renounced their share in the land of Canaan.   Nevertheless, while still uncircumcised, they actually entered into the land : and they not only thus *practically* took possession of it, but even formally received the *investiture* of it from God himself†.   No doubt,

* The Afghans, the Ten Tribes, p. 47, 48, 49.
† Joshua. i.

E

Circumcision was renewed *after* they had passed the Jordan : but this circumstance could not do away facts which had *already* occurred*.

I may add, that the present argument destroys itself.

If the rite of Circumcision, in addition to the rite of Baptism, be requisite to the possession of Canaan by the Ten Tribes, or in truth by the whole Twelve Tribes, when converted and restored : then, not only is the entire analogy of the Gospel violated, but Scripture itself is directly contradicted.

Stand fast, says St. Paul, *in the liberty wherewith Christ hath made us free : and be not entangled again in the yoke of Bondage. Behold, I Paul say unto you : that if ye be circumcised, Christ shall profit you nothing*†.

Yet the very argument before us, which makes Circumcision the covenanted condition of possessing the land of Canaan, plainly requires, that, with the converted and restored Israelites, Circumcision should never cease to be obligatory. Nevertheless, it is worthy of note, that, in none of the various prophecies, which describe the condition of the Israelites after their restoration, is there any

* Joshua. v. 2–9.   † Galat. v. 1. 2.

mention of their retaining the rite of Circumcision*.

(3.) As for the third objection, we may reasonably say, that it is dangerous to oppose a specula-
tive probability to a recorded fact.

To Sir George's probability, the express historical testimony of Scripture stands in direct
antagonism.

The first detachment of Israelites was deported
exclusively to Assyria : at least, neither Media
nor any other country, is mentioned†.

The second, described collectively as *Israel*,
was also carried away into Assyria, and was
locally placed in Halah and by Habor the river of
Gozan : but, that region being now filled up by the
new occupants, some individuals that still remained
were placed in certain cities of Media; which
cities must obviously have been in that western
part of Media that bordered on Assyria, and
which, like Assyria, seems, in the oriental fashion,
to have been rendered vacant by the extermination
or at least the transplantation of the former
inhabitants‡.

* Compare Isaiah. lx. lxvi. ; Jerem. xxxi. ; Ezek. xxxvi.
xxxvii. ; Zechar. xiv.

† 2 Kings. xv. 29.　　　　　‡ 2 Kings. xvii. 5, 6.

Here we have, I submit, a record of distinct FACTS : and we cannot safely allow them to be set aside, merely because it is *conjectured,* that policy would forbid the planting of a nation, *supposed* indeed to be turbulent, but *much more probably* broken in spirit by recent calamity, in a mountainous and difficult country. I may add, that Sir George's own general description of Media, as *a rich and populous province,* is irreconcilable with his conjecture. If Media were *already* rich and populous in its general character, the deported Israelites, as a body, could not have been placed in a *then* fully occupied country, simply because there would have been no room for them.

3. After all, it is scarcely worth while to dispute, whether Dr. Grant's opinion is tenable or untenable.

Let the Nestorians be what they may, there is quite sufficient evidence, that a remnant of the deported Ten Tribes still occupies the scripturally declared land of their original deportation. Dr. Grant himself attests, that a considerable body of religionists occupy the country conjointly with the Nestorians. These adhere to the Law of Moses and to the Levitical Ordinances : and, upon them, Dr. Grant, somewhat inaccurately

according to his own statements, bestows the
name of *Jews;* for he very rightly, in my
judgment, deems them *Israelites* of the Ten Tribes.
That such is their true character, I make no
doubt: for every thing tends to establish it.
They are dwelling in the very land, whither
Scripture assures us the Ten Tribes were deported: and the existence of the Ten Tribes there
in the days of Josephus and Jerome, that is to
say, in the first century and in the fifth century,
is distinctly asserted by both those writers. I
have already given the statements of Josephus,
and have briefly noticed the testimony of Jerome
to the same effect. It may not be useless,
however, to give the precise words of the latter
witness.

*We read, that the Ten Tribes were led away
captive by Phul and Salmanassar and Teglath-
Phalassar, Kings of the Assyrians, aud that they
are still in captivity there even* UNTO THE PRESENT
DAY[*].

UNTO THE PRESENT DAY, *the Ten Tribes are*

---

[*] Legimus Decem Tribus captas a Phul et Salmanassar et
Teglath-Phalassar regibus Assyriorum, et USQUE HODIE ibi
esse captivas.— Hieron. Comment. in Ezek. xvi. 55. Oper.
tom. iv. p. 378–379.

*held captive, in the mountains, and in the cities of
the Medes, to which they had been deported**.

The Ten Tribes, which were called Israel, EVEN
UNTO THE PRESENT DAY *are servilely captive, in
the mountains, and in the cities of the Medes*†.

Putting then the Nestorians out of the question,
and admitting for the sake of argument that Dr.
Robinson has been completely successful in con-
futing the opinion of Dr. Grant that they are a
remnant of the Ten Tribes long since converted
to Christianity, it appears to me, that the joint
testimonies of Josephus and Jerome relative to

---

* USQUE HODIE Decem Tribus captivæ teneantur, in montibus, et in urbibus Medorum, ad quas translatæ sunt.   Comment. in Ezek. xxiii. 1.   Oper. tom. iv. p. 399.

† Decem Tribus, quæ vocabantur *Israel*, USQUE HODIE, in
montibus, urbibusque Medorum, servire captivas.   Comment.
in Ezek. xxxvii. 15.   Oper. tom. iv. p. 447.

In my construction of these passages, I disjoin *montibus*
from *urbibus Medorum*.   The *mountains* are the mountainous
district of Assyria, the geography of which is settled by the
mention of the river Habor or Chabour: the *cities* are the
cities or pagi of western Media.

Jerome speaks to the same effect, though not quite so
precisely, in another place.

Neque Decem Tribus, quæ in civitatibus Medorum EXULANT
atque Persarum, reversas in terram Judæam legimus.   Comment in Hieron. xxxi. 16.   Oper. tom. iv. p. 298.

The proof here lies in the present tense EXULANT: they are
NOW exiles.

the still continued existence of the Ten Tribes, or at least a portion of them, in Adiabenè when they wrote, and the harmonising FACT that at the present day there is still a body of Hebrews in the same country, answer to each other like the two edges of an indenture : and thus, even if Dr. Grant be mistaken in regard to the nationality of the Nestorians, we have as full a proof as can be expected, that a remnant of the Ten Tribes still exists in the very country, whither Scripture declares them to have been deported, and where, accordingly, they must, in the first instance, be sought for.

4. Yet they are not to be sought *exclusively* in Assyria and Media.

Mr. Layard remarks : that, *Amongst the Jewish Population scattered widely over this part of ancient Media, might be sought the descendants of the Ten Tribes with more probability, than in the various lands which ingenious speculation had pointed out as the dwelling-places of the remnant of Israel*.

He is speaking of the lofty country not far from the great lake Van, which, in an extended

* Layard's Discoveries in the Ruins of Nineveh and Babylon, p. 386, note.

sense, may perhaps be deemed a part of ancient Media: and his view would have been correct, had he not, by the force of his comparison, *limited* the Ten Tribes to that particular region. Here he is in error. That a *part* of the Ten Tribes must be there, I feel no doubt: because the very necessity of Prophecy requires it. Isaiah declares, that they will be restored *out of* Assyria. Therefore, they must now be *in* Assyria. But then, according to the same prophet, Assyria is not the *only* country out of which they are to be gathered. He additionally specifies various other eastern regions, as the districts whence they are to return, and therefore as the districts where they are now to be sought: Cush or the Asiatic Ethiopia, Elam or Persia, Shinar or Babylonia, Hamath or a region bordering on northern Canaan*. Hence we may conclude, that, by numerous successive emigrations from Assyria and Media, the descendants of the Ten Tribes may now be found throughout the greater part of at least southern Asia.

5. It may be proper to remark, that, in the preceding statements, I would not be understood to deny that Dr. Grant *may* be correct in his

* Isaiah. xi. 11–16.

view of the Israelitish Origin of the Nestorians. I would merely say, that those, whom he calls Jews, though he describes them as being *Israelites,* form a less disputable and therefore a more unobjectionable medium of proof, that a remnant of the Ten Tribes still remain in the land of their first deportation.

XII. Sir George Rose himself contends : that the Afghans are the descendants, and (as I understand him) the *exclusive* descendants of the Ten Tribes.

1. This opinion, as to the origin of the Afghans, was first, I believe, brought forward, in the year 1784, by Mr. Vansittart in a letter to Sir William Jones*.

Certain objections to it, Sir George very ably disposes of : and I see no reason, why it may not be adopted, as at least highly probable, though it does not possess the sort of certainty involved in a scripturally well-defined country†. The fault of

* See Asiatic Researches. vol. ii. p. 67–76.

† When Mr. Vansittart's Translation of a Persian Abridgment of the *Asrarul Afaghinah* was transmitted to Sir William Jones, he strongly recommended an inquiry into the literature and history of the Afghans. In one speculation, however, the learned President strikes me as having been mistaken.

We learn from Esdras, he says, *that the Ten Tribes, after a wandering journey, came to a country called* ARSARETH :

Sir George's Work is, not the opinion that the Afghans are descendants of the Ten Tribes, but the implication contained in the propounding of another opinion : the opinion, namely, that the present inhabitants of the ancient land of Ashur, whither, as a *Fact*, we know the Ten Tribes to have been deported, are *not* their descendants.

2. Dr. Grant remarks, that the Christian Population of Assyria and the adjoining western district of Media may not be far short of 200,000.

Sir George thinks, that this, even alone, is conclusive against Dr. Grant's opinion, inasmuch as he *offers a maximum of 200,000, as the* WHOLE *of the progeny of the Ten Tribes.*

where, we may suppose, they settled.—A considerable district under the dominion of the Afghans is called HAZAREH *or* HAZARET, *which might easily have been changed into the word used by Esdras.*   Asiat. Res. vol. ii. p. 76.

The conjecture is *etymologically* ingenious : but it fails, both *circumstantially* and *geographically*.

Circumstantially : because, as it has since been learned, Hazaret is only a *recent* conquest of the Afghans.

Geographically : because, being on the confines of western Hindostan, it is irreconcileable with the locality to which Esdras conducts the Ten Tribes by crossing the narrow passages of the Euphrates, and proceeding thence in the same direction to a land uninhabited.

The *Arsareth* of Esdras is, I think, pretty plainly *Ararath* or *Armenia*.

I did not understand Dr. Grant to make any such assertion. He appeared to me to say, that this was about the *present* Christian population of the country into which the Ten Tribes were deported: and, possibly, the unconverted population may be about the same. Now this is a very good reason for supposing, that various colonies have gone forth from the parent stock when the tyrannical pressure of the mighty Assyrian Empire was removed by its overthrow: and thence, it affords a strong collateral argument for the Israelitic origin of the Afghans; because it is quite clear, that the whole progeny of the Ten Tribes cannot be confined to 200,000, or even 400,000. But I see not, how it at all aids Sir George, in overthrowing the opinion of Dr. Grant, and in establishing (as I understand him) the *exclusive* right of the Afghans to be deemed the Children of the Ten Tribes.

3. In truth, Sir George, by his management of a probably correct opinion, brings out a result contradictory alike to Scripture and to Geography.

He finds himself compelled to make the country of the Afghans, or rather the first of the successive countries which they occupied in their

progress eastward, to be the region, whither the
Ten Tribes were originally deported. Now Scripture assures us, that this region was Assyria and
a neighbouring district of Media. But Sir George,
suppressing all mention of Assyria, would make
Media alone the land to which the Ten Tribes
were deported : and, at the same time, supposes,
that they must have crossed the Euphrates not
far from the middle point of the course of the
river. Now such a local transit would bring them
far too much south for the greater part of even
Media : and, at the same time, it would be quite
out of their line of march to the still laterally
more northern province of Ashur ; for the due
reaching of which province they must, as the
apocryphal Esdras speaks, have crossed by the
narrow passages of the river ; that is to say, considerably higher up the stream.

To meet this difficulty, which springs immediately out of the very plain scriptural account,
he tells us, that the extensive province of modern
Khorassan is known as identical with the Media
of ancient Geography.

But, even if such a statement were strictly
accurate, we should still have in it a total omission
of Ashur. And yet Ashur, from the mode in

which it is mentioned, is evidently the chief land of the deportation : for the cities of the Medes are only subjoined supplementally.

I doubt, however, whether it *is* geographically accurate.

In order to form some judgment on the question, I compared a map of ancient geography with the excellent modern map of Persia in the Atlas published (I believe) under the inspection of the late eminent Sir John Barrow : and, from that comparison, I drew out, as faithfully as I could, a result fatal to the assertion of Sir George Rose.

So far from the modern Khorassan coinciding with ancient Media, Khorassan, from a comparison of my two maps, lies directly east of Media, and *commences* where ancient Media *terminated* : for the eastern boundary of ancient Media loosely corresponds with the fifty-third degree of East Longitude; and this, so far as I can make out the comparison, is the very degree of East Longitude where the western boundary of modern Khorassan loosely commences*.

* I reduced, as well as I could, the reckoning of East Longitude from the Fortunate Islands to the reckoning of the same Longitude from Greenwich.

To suppose, then, that, even if Media had been the exclusive region into which the Ten Tribes were deported, they would *therefore* have been, by Shalmaneser, deported into modern Khorassan, is, unless either my maps mislead me or I have totally misunderstood them, a plain impossibility.

4. But let us only follow the scriptural statement, and all will be abundantly clear.

The Ten Tribes were originally planted, partly in the then unpeopled province of Ashur, and partly in certain cities of the western part of Media. From this locality, the germ of the Afghan Colony (for I am far from denying the Afghans to be Israelites) would pass eastward through the whole breadth of Media into Khorassan : and thence, as Sir George very well traces them, through Caubul and Cashmere, into their present settlement on the borders of Hindostan.

Hence, provided these distinctions are observed, and provided we give up the untenable scheme of making Khorassan the country in which they were *first* planted when deported from Samaria, I see no reason to reject, or rather indeed much reason to adopt, the opinion, that the Afghans are descended from the Ten Tribes, though they may not be the *sole* descendants.

XIII. In accordance with the opinion of Dr.
Buchanan, various colonies of Israelites seem to
be existing throughout nearly the whole of Asia.

1. This is stated by him as a fact.

In Cashmere, Tartary, Persia, Cochin, and
Malabar, allied Communities of Israelites have
been discovered, who appear to have been separated from the primitive stock, long before the
last dispersion of the Jews properly so called,
and indeed before the time of the Babylonian
Captivity. These Communities, though, by successive migrations in the course of so many centuries, they are now geographically separated from
each other, are said, still, by letters and occasional visits, to keep up a mutual intercourse and
connexion*.

2. A question may be raised, whether some of
these are Jews, or whether they be fragments of
the Ten Tribes.

Dr. Buchanan tells us, that, at Cochin, there is
a colony of Jews, who retain the tradition that
they arrived in India soon after the Babylonian
Captivity. There are, it seems, in that province,
two classes of Jews: the white Jews and the
black Jews. The black Jews are those, who are

* See Buchanan's Christian Researches. p. 310–324.

supposed to have arrived at that early period: the white Jews emigrated from Europe in later ages. What seems to countenance the tradition of the black Jews is, that they have copies of those books of the Old Testament which were written previously to the Captivity, but none whose dates are subsequent to that event*.

The tradition of the black Jews is, no doubt, of some importance: but the greater part of the Books of the Old Testament, that were written before the Babylonian Captivity, might, so far as dates are concerned, have been possessed by the deported Ten Tribes as well as by Jewish emigrants from Babylon. This part of the evidence, therefore, leaves it doubtful, whether the so-called black Jews of Cochin are descended from the Two Tribes or from the Ten Tribes.

3. As far as I can judge, there is something of the same doubtfulness respecting an extraordinary Hebrew colony in China.

A very curious and interesting account of them has been published by Mr. Finn, under the title of *The Jews in China*: and he himself believes them to be Jews, not Israelites of the Ten Tribes.

---

* Buchanan's Memoir on an Indian Ecclesiastical Establishment. p. 117, 118.

His argument to prove them Jews of the Restoration from Chaldea strikes me as not being perfectly conclusive.

It is based upon their knowledge of Ezra, the second lawgiver and reformer of the people, who flourished *after* the captivity of the Ten Tribes by Shalmaneser, and likewise upon their possession of some portions of the Sacred Books, which similarly were written *after* their deportation into Assyria.

I must confess, that I see very little force in this argument. He himself admits, that its cogency may be abated, by taking into account, that, for several centuries, their Sacred Books and some of their teachers might have reached them from another country in the West, and by thence concluding that thus only may have been imported the later Scriptures and the knowledge of Ezra. But he adds: *This conclusion is entirely gratuitous, without evidence of even the lowest degree.*

Now, that there is no existing evidence to that effect, may be perfectly true: but it forms only a narrow basis for a valid argument. The forgetting a matter in the lapse of many centuries, even if among the *more lettered* part of the community it

F

has really been forgotten, is no proof that it never occurred: and, most evidently, Father Ricci's visitor was not *judaically* lettered. But let that pass. Mr. Finn allows it to be plain, that this Chinese Colony *must*, from the circumstance of their ignorance of the name JESUS until it was mentioned to them by the missionaries, be a very ancient offshoot: and thence he lays it down, that they had branched off, not from the Ten Tribes, but from the restored Jews of Jerusalem *anterior* to the Incarnation of Christ.

That they had branched off from the parent stock anterior to the Incarnation, is plain enough from their ignorance of the very name of JESUS: but this is no proof, as Mr. Finn's language seems evidently to import, either that they *must have been* an offshoot from the Jews of Jerusalem after their return from the Babylonian Captivity, or that they *could not have been* an offshoot from the deported Ten Tribes. Their ignorance of the name of JESUS would simply leave the matter open to either supposition: because such ignorance would simply demonstrate the fact, that they *must* have emigrated into China when they had no knowledge of the name; a circumstance which would apply to the one hypothesis just as

well as to the other. They *might* have left Judea
without any knowledge of the name: but then
they might *equally* have left Assyria without any
knowledge of it.

In short, the weakness of Mr. Finn's argument
to show that they *must* be Jews and *could not* be
Israelites of the Ten Tribes, will fully appear if
we advert to the case of those undoubted Israelites
who are intermixed with the Nestorians in Assyria
and Media, the very region whither their ancestors
were transported by Pul and Tiglath-Pileser and
Shalmaneser.   Dr. Grant tells us, that they deny
themselves to be descendants of Judah, because
*they claim to be a part of the Ten Tribes carried
away captive by the Kings of Assyria :* and, when
we consider the country which they still inhabit,
there cannot, I think, be a reasonable doubt that
their claim is just.   Historical Tradition and
Actual Geography concur in establishing it.   Yet,
so far from being ignorant of the name of JESUS,
they were so well acquainted with it, and thence
we may presume equally acquainted with the
Books of Scripture which were written after the
deportation of their ancestors, that, acknowledging (as Dr. Grant asserts) the Nestorians to be
Israelites like themselves, they bitterly hated

them on the ground, that they had apostatised from the Ancient Faith in the days of Christ and his Apostles.

Now, in what manner could this remnant of the Ten Tribes have acquired such knowledge?

Clearly and obviously, it must have been conveyed to them from their brethren of the House of Judah, with whom, according to the testimony of Josephus, they ceased not to keep up a perpetual intercourse.

But, if *they* received the knowledge by communication, there can be no reason why the Chinese Colony may not *similarly* have received *their* knowledge of Ezra and *their* acquaintance with portions of the Sacred Books written *after* the captivity of the Ten Tribes. This is made the more likely from the fact stated by Dr. Buchanan, that various colonies of Israelites are in existence throughout nearly the whole of Asia, who, by letters and occasional visits, still keep up a mutual intercourse and connexion.

After all that can be said on either side, it must remain a matter of some doubt whether this Colony of Hebrews in China is composed of Jews or of Israelites. So far as I can judge, the preponderance of evidence is in favour of the latter

supposition.   I would not build too confidently
upon their ignorance of the name JESUS; because
that would be equally accounted for, whether they
were a fragment of the Ten Tribes or emigrants of
the House of Judah prior to the Incarnation: but
it is difficult to comprehend how a Colony of Jews
could have been ignorant of the very name of
JEW, and yet should have well remembered and
retained the appellation of ISRAELITE.   Such,
nevertheless, was actually the case.   When they
first became known to the Jesuit Missionaries at
the beginning of the seventeenth century, one of
them, who visited Father Ricci at Pekin, styled
himself an ISRAELITE, and knew nothing of any
such name as JEW.

In the year 1816, Dr. Morrison heard of them
from a Mohammedan near Pekin, as subsisting in
Kae-fung-foo under the old name bestowed upon
them by the Chinese.   They were still called *The
Religion of Cutting out the Sinew:* an appellation,
as Mr. Finn justly observes, so appropriately
Israelitish in every Branch of Israel, that, if the
name were assumed by any other people than the
descendants of Jacob, it would be impossible for
them to assign a satisfactory reason for its origination.

Among the various signs of the times, is the semi-Christian rebellion of the native Chinese against the intrusive Tartar Dynasty. Some anticipate from it the establishment of sound Christianity : others set it down as a delusion analogous to the Mormon Imposture. Whatever be its true character, it may tend to throw some further light upon this remarkable Colony of Hebrews.*

XIV. Distinct apparently from all the fragments, noticed either by Dr. Buchanan or Mr. Finn; the senior missionary to the Jews, Mr. Samuel, discovered what he supposed to be the Two Tribes and a Half on the western shore of the Caspian Sea.

As this locality is not very far distant, northward, from Assyria, it is not improbable that the Two Tribes and a Half, deported by Pul and Tiglath-Pileser into Ashur, may have been subsequently moved northward, to the western shore of the Caspian, by Shalmaneser, for the purpose of acquiring more room in Ashur, whither he subsequently carried away the remaining Seven Tribes and a Half : and this is rendered the more

* For some further remarks on this interesting subject, see Appendix.

likely from the circumstance that some of the captive Israelites were planted in the cities of the Medes ; which implies that there was still a want of room in Ashur.

Those, whom Mr. Samuel found on the western shore of the Caspian, had not been converted to Christianity : and they were readily known to be Israelites by their continuing to observe the usages of the Ceremonial Law. Like the Nestorians of Assyria and their still unconverted brethren, if *really* brethren, they were shut up in the midst of barbarous tribes : and, along with them, they occupied the mountainous region of Daghistan, which extends about 134 miles in length and between 30 and 40 in breadth. The Lesghies, who are, however, bigoted Mohammedans, affirm themselves to be descended from the Tribe of Dan : and, in many respects, their physiognomy and character assimilate to the Hebrew. Curiously enough, they acknowledge those who retain the Law of Moses to be the original inhabitants of the mountains : although they themselves appear to be of the same stock, and, so far as outward figure goes, to be descended from common parents.

This discovery of the Ten Tribes, at the present important crisis, says Mr. Samuel, must appear a wonderful event. The preservation of them through so many ages, in the very heart of their enemies, must be acknowledged as a most signal act of Divine Providence : and we need no stronger or more convincing proof of the Time of their Restoration being at hand; when they shall be taken from the place of their interment for near two thousand five hundred years, and be restored to their own land, to share with their brethren of the House of Judah the splendour of the Messiah's kingdom*.

XV. I have remarked, that the Hebrews found by Mr. Samuel on the western shore of the Caspian, had probably been removed thither by Shalmaneser, from want of room in Upper Assyria and the cities of the Medes. This probability is increased by one of the sculptured historical slabs disinterred by Mr. Layard from the Ninevite Mound of Kouyunjik. The particulars will be most fitly given in the words of that gentleman himself.

Above the Assyrian warriors, were the captives and their torturers. The former differed in costume

---

* Remnant found, p. 107, 108. See also, ibid. p. xii.–xiv. 42–47.

from the Susinian fighting-men represented in the adjoining bas-reliefs. They were distinguished by the smallness of their stature and by a very marked Jewish countenance: a sharp hooked nose, short bushy beard, and long narrow eyes. Could they have belonged to the Hebrew Tribes, which were carried away from Samaria, and placed by Shalmaneser, Sennacherib, or Esar-Haddon, as colonists in the distant regions of Elam, and who, having become powerful in their new settlements, had revolted against their Assyrian rulers, and were once again subdued?—Some, in iron fetters, were in the act of being led before the king, for judgment or pardon. Others had been condemned to the torture, and were already in the hands of the executioners. —Above these groups was a short epigraph, commencing by two determinative signs of proper names, each followed by a blank space, which the sculptor probably left to be filled up with the names of the principal victims. It then declares, that these men, having spoken blasphemies against Asshur the great god of the Assyrians, their tongues had been pulled out (LISHANESHUNU ESHLUP, both words being almost purely Hebrew), and that they had afterwards been put to death or tortured. The inscription, therefore, corresponds

with the sculpture beneath. It is by such confir-
matory evidence that the accuracy of the transla-
tions of the cuneiform characters may be tested*.

On this curious statement, I may be allowed to
make two confirmatory remarks.

1. Elam is one of the oriental countries out of
which, as well as out of Assyria, the Israelites, as
we are taught by Isaiah, are destined to be re-
stored†: and, though some might be barbarously
put to death by Sennacherib, we can scarcely
suppose that such would be the fate of all.

2. The crime, for which the unfortunate ring-
leaders were tortured and slain, is precisely that
which might have been characteristically alleged
against an Israelite, and which is greatly eluci-
dated by the sentence which Nebuchadnezzar
pronounced upon the three young Hebrews for
refusing to serve the gods of the king, and to
worship the golden image which he had set up.
It was blasphemy against the great god Asshur,
the deified ancestor of the Assyrians : who, on
the general principle of Paganism, received, as
a Demon or Hero-god, the worship of his
descendants.

---

* Layard's Nineveh and Babylon, p. 456, 458.
† Isaiah. xi. 11.

It may be additionally remarked, that the Hebraistic inscription, setting forth the appropriate punishment of those who were deemed blasphemers, seems very evidently to sustain Mr. Layard's reasonable conjecture that the culprits were individuals of the deported Ten Tribes.

XVI. In times like the present, such discoveries are most deeply interesting. Yet is the interest of a very awful description.

If we be drawing near to the Dissolution of the Ottoman Power, and to the subsequent Restoration of Israel and Judah, and thence also to the close of the fated 1260 years: we must, of plain prophetic necessity, be also drawing near to that unexampled time of trouble, which is universally and unanimously foretold, as synchronising with the Return of God's Ancient People, and as effecting the final downfall of that baneful Apostatic Perversion of Christianity, which is described as making one vigorous effort to recover its usurped authority, ere, like a millstone, it sinks irremediably into the abyss of utter perdition.

May this Protestant Country retrace its steps before it be too late: lest it, partaking as it has fearfully done in the sins of the mystic Babylon, should receive also of her destined plagues. May it, through God's undeserved mercy, be preserved from a return to, or an encouragement of the delusive errors, which it renounced in the day of the blessed Reformation!

It has been alleged, I understand, that, if we judge from their conduct, the Turks are somewhat better Christians than the Czar and his Russians.

I am not at all disposed to controvert this view: for I deem the behaviour of the latter most infamous. But *this* is not precisely the question. I treated my subject *prophetically*, not *morally:* and so I desire to be understood.

Agreeably to every just rule of application, the overthrow of Turkey is most clearly announced under the Sixth Apocalyptic Vial: and, accordingly, on this point, there has been a remarkable agreement among our best commentators.

The *general* time of its occurrence is, I think, pretty clearly placed *before* the expiration of the 1260 years: but the *precise* year is undetermined.

That Turkey, however, is a doomed State, I have no doubt: and I think, that its Fall is not very distant. As for the *character* of Russia, we have no concern with *that*. God perpetually accomplishes his purposes of judgment by the instrumentality of Powers, *the rods of his anger,* which are the very reverse of what is good : and, if Turkey falls by the agency of Russia, the circumstance will simply be in close analogy with the ordinary proceedings of the Deity. Politicians must act from *circumstances,* according to the best of their honest judgment. The application of Prophecy, as a *guide* to public measures, is an entire departure from *sound principle.* From Prophecy, I gather, that Turkey will, ere long, fall; and thus make way for the Restoration of Israel : and I believe, still from Prophecy, that its Downfall will produce that fearful war, which is the subject of all predictions that treat of these latter times. But the opinion of a *commentator* is no ruling guide to *politicians :* nor do I conceive, that Christian governments (so called) would be guilty of any breach of morals by aiding Turkey against the clearly unprincipled aggressions of Russia.

I hope I am now sufficiently understood. As I treat it, the subject is not *moral,* but purely *prophetical.*

Oct. 12, 1853.

APPENDIX.

As yet, we know so little definitely of the mighty revolution which is now progressing in China, that no sober person would venture to pronounce positively upon either its results or its consequences.

Its leader, who (I believe) politically claims to be the representative and true heir of the ancient Royal Chinese Dynasty which was supplanted by the intrusive Tartars, claims also, it is said, to be the herald of what might seem to be a new revelation.

He and his followers profess Christianity untainted by the novelties and absurdities of Popery: but, if there be any truth in the statement, which exhibits him as styling himself and as being styled by his adherents the *Younger Brother of Jesus Christ*, it is difficult to refrain from mistrusting the soundness of his Theology.

Yet it is only fair to remark, that such phraseology is capable of an innocent sense. Our Lord himself declares, that his disciples are his *brethren*: and the very circumstance of his Incarnation as set forth in Scripture makes him, if we may so speak, our elder brother and near kinsman; whence we are called *members of his body, his flesh, and his bones*. The expression, therefore, *may* be used innocently. Peradventure, also, it may be used distinctively, as marking the difference between an intended modest title and the arrogance of him who was wont to style himself the *Brother of the Sun and Moon*. At all events, if the native claimant of the throne calls himself the *Younger Brother of Christ*, he is likewise said specially to prohibit all adoration of himself and any application to him of the titles and attributes of the Deity. On the whole, it is the part of wisdom to wait and see the progress and result of this extraordinary movement, before we adventure any direct opinion upon it.

Should Tae-Ping-Wang prove a Chinese Constantine, his success cannot but exercise a mighty influence westward. He may be the destined subverter of the wide-spread superstition of Buddhism, and, conjunctively with the nations of Europe, the destroyer of Mohammedism in Persia and Eastern Turkey. Thus, when the waters of the mystic Euphrates are completely dried up, China may become a mighty agent in working out that way for the kings from the Rising of the Sun which will be prepared by the Downfall of the Ottoman Power.

As yet, we know but very imperfectly what numbers of the Hebrews of the Ten Tribes may be concealed in the unexplored recesses of that immense Empire. That *some* Hebrews are there, whether Jews or Israelites, we *do* know. Mr. Finn, as we have seen, deems them Jews. The weight of evidence, contained in *his own* very graphical statements, inclines me to think it more probable that they are Israelites of the Ten Tribes. I subjoin, however, his statement in full, that so each person may be enabled to judge for himself on which side probability preponderates.

" The Jesuit Missionaries were but a short time settled in Pe-king, when, one summer's day at the beginning of the seventeenth century, a visitor called upon Father Matthew Ricci, induced to do so by an account, then recently published in the metropolis, of the foreigners who worshipped a single Lord of Heaven and Earth, and who yet were not Mohammedans. Entering the house with a smile, he announced himself as one of the same religion with its inmates. The Missionary, remarking how much his features and figure differed from those prevailing among the Chinese, led him to the chapel. It was St. John Baptist's day: and, over the altar, was a painting of the Virgin Mary with the infant Jesus and the future Baptist on his knees before them. The stranger bowed to the picture as Ricci did: but explained, at the same time, that he was not accustomed to do so before any such representations; only he could not refrain from paying the usual homage of the country to his great ancestors. Beside the altar, were pictures of the four Evangelists. He inquired, if these were not of the twelve? Ricci answered in the affirmative, supposing him to mean the Twelve Apostles. Then, returning to the first apartment, he proposed questions in turn: and an unexpected explanation ensued. The stranger was a descendant of Israel: and, during his survey of the chapel, had imagined the large picture to represent Rebekah with Jacob and Esau, and the other persons to denote four of the sons of Jacob.

" It was some time before this simple explanation could be elicited, on account of the misunderstanding on both sides, which impeded the use of direct interrogation. The visitor, however, knew nothing of the appellation JEW. He styled himself AN ISRAELITE, by name Ngai, a native of Kae-fung-foo, the capital of the province Honan, where, having prepared himself by study for a Mandarin degree, he had now repaired to Pe-king for his examination : and, led by curiosity or fellow-feeling for the supposed fraternity of his nation, he had thus ventured to call at the mission-house.

" He stated, that, in his native city, there were ten or twelve families of Israelites, with a fair synagogue, which they had recently restored and decorated at the expense of ten thousand crowns, and in which they preserved a roll of the Law four or five hundred years old : adding, that, in Hang-chow-foo, the capital of Chekeang, there were considerably more families with their synagogue.

" He made several allusions to events and persons of Scripture-History: but pronounced the names differently from the mode usual in Europe. When shewn a Hebrew Bible, he was unable to read it, though he at once recognised the characters. He said, that Hebrew learning was still

maintained among his people, and that his brother was a proficient in it: and he seemed to
confess, that his own neglect of it, with a preference for gentile literature, had exposed him to
censure from the congregation and the rabbi:
but this gave him little concern, as his ambition
aimed at the honours to be gained from Chinese
learning; a disciple rather of Confutius than of
Moses.

"Three years afterwards, having had no earlier
opportunity, Ricci despatched a Chinese Christian
to investigate, at Kae-fung-foo, the truth of this
singular discovery. All was found to be as described: and the messenger brought back with
him a copy of the titles and endings of the Five
Books of Moses. These were compared with the
Plantinian Bible, and found to correspond exactly:
the writing, however, had no vowel points. Ricci,
ignorant of Hebrew, commissioned the same native
convert to return with an epistle in Chinese, addressed to the Rabbi: announcing, that, at Pe-
king, he was possessor of all the other Books of
the Old Testament, as well as those of the New
Testament; which contains a record of the acts of
Messiah, who is already come. In reply, the
Rabbi asserted: that Messiah is not only not

come, but that he would not appear for ten thousand years. He added, that he would willingly transfer to him the government of the synagogue, if Ricci would abstain from swine's flesh and reside with the community.

" Afterwards, arrived three Israelites together from the same city, apparently willing to receive Christianity. One of these was son of the brother (already mentioned) of the first visitor. They were received with kindness, and instructed in many things of which their Rabbis were ignorant: and, when taught the history of Christ, they all paid to his image the same adoration as their entertainers did. Some books being given to them in the Chinese language, such as *A Compendium of Christian Faith* and others of the same nature, they read them, and carried them home on their return.—

" These personages readily fell in with several opinions of the missionaries. They expressed a desire for pictures as helps to devotion to be in their synagogue and private oratories, particularly for pictures of Jesus. They complained of the interdiction from slaughtering animals for themselves: which if they had not transgressed recently upon the road, they must have perished with

hunger. They were likewise ready to renounce
the rite of circumcision on the eighth day, which
their wives and the surrounding heathen de-
nounced as a barbarous and cruel practice. And
they held out the expectation, that, inasmuch as
Christianity offers relief in such matters, it would
be easily adopted among their people. Yet the
author gives no account of any consequent con-
versions. He passes on abruptly from this subject
of *Jewish Filth* to relate the progress of *Christian
Truth* in China.

" It appeared, on further inquiry, that the
Chinese comprise, under the one designation
Hwuy-hwuy, the three religions, of Israelites,
Mohammedans, and Cross-worshippers : the last,
descendants of early Syrian Christians, subsisting
in certain provinces.

" They distinguish them thus :

" 1. The Mohammedans, as the *Hwuy* ab-
staining from pork :

" 2. The Israelites, as the *Hwuy* who cut out
the nerves and sinews from their meat :

" 3. The Cross-worshippers, as the *Hwuy* who
refuse to eat of animals which have an undivided
hoof : which latter restriction, it was said, the
Israelites there did not observe.

" Julius Aleni, after the death of Ricci, being a Hebrew scholar, visited Kae-fung-foo about the year 1613 : but found circumstances so much changed from some cause or other, that, although he entered the synagogue and admired its cleanliness, they would not withdraw the curtains which concealed the sacred books.

" In Nan-king, Semmedo was informed by a Mohammedan, that, in that city, he knew of four families of Jews who had embraced the religion of the Koran, they being the last of their race there, and their instructors having failed as their numbers diminished.

" Indeed, the visitors from Kae-fung-foo had before assured Ricci, in Pe-king, that the same cause would soon reduce them to the alternative of becoming either Heathens or Mohammedans.

" However, Semmedo, writing in 1642, consoled himself with the hope, that, whereas a Christian church had been recently erected in that city, the congregation of the synagogue would rather receive Christianity : which, besides the consideration of its being the truth, is most nearly allied to their own religion.—

" Such was the amount of intelligence received in Europe concerning that remote off-shoot of

Israel up to the middle of the seventeenth century. Christendom was not unconcerned at the discovery. China itself was but a newly-opened mine for European research. The indistinct glimpses, afforded by Marco Polo in the thirteenth century, were indeed extending into broader fields of vision, by means of the obedient zeal of Romanist missionaries: but, when Xavier, expiring within sight of China before admission was conceded to Christianity, prayed for its conversion with his latest accents; and when Valignano so frequently turned his looks from Macao toward the prohibited land, exclaiming, *O rock, rock, when wilt thou open?* they were not aware, that, within that strong solidity, was to be found a relic of the peculiar nation who are everywhere witnesses of *the goodness and severity of God.*

" The devout rejoiced at this fresh demonstration of Scripture Truth respecting the scattered yet guarded race. The philosophical marvelled at the fact of a Mosaic People, so ancient as to be ignorant of the denomination JEW; emigrants out of Empires now long since extinct, into a very different phasis of civilisation, but preserved with their old language and religion even to these days : and, moreover, that, with so slight efforts made, these should be known to exist, at four various points, containing a line of seven hundred miles, from Pe-king to Hang-chow-foo. But, perhaps, no class of men felt greater concern in the event than the laborious biblical critics of the time. To them, the finding of some of that nation, *to whom were committed the oracles of God,* yet supposed to be of too ancient a separation to be cognizant of either the Samaritan or the Septuagint or the Masoretic texts of the Old Testament, yet still guarding their copies of the Law of Moses, was a circumstance most pregnant with hopeful interest : and the more a matter of anxiety, as those Israelites were represented as almost ceasing to subsist; and there was great possibility, that, with the failure of Hebrew reading consequent on the adoption of a novel creed, the manuscripts themselves might be suffered to perish. The subject was referred to, in the Prolegomena (iii. § 41), of Walton's Polyglott Bible, and in the Preface to Jablonski's Hebrew Bible (§ 38); and further information as to the text of the Chinese Copies of the Pentateuch was ardently desired.—

" From the communication of Gozani, it appears: that, in 1702, he had intended to visit the *Taou-kin-keaou*, that is, the *Sect who cut out the sinew*, as the Israelites were expressively designated; but was deterred by some imaginary obstacles, and by the real difficulty in his ignorance of the Hebrew language. Two years afterwards, he had resumed the task in obedience to instructions sent out from Rome. He commenced by advancing certain civilities. In return, they visited him. And then he proceeded to their synagogue, the distance being only that of a few streets: where he found them assembled. They showed him their religious books: and even led him to the most sacred parts of the edifice, to which only the Rabbi has right of access. With great politeness, they gave him all the explanations he requested, as to their Scriptures, their history, and their religious ceremonies. On the walls, he perceived inscriptions both in Chinese and in Hebrew. These they permitted him to copy: and he despatched the copies, with his letter, to Rome. The whole reception testified, that the unfriendliness of the last half century between the neighbours was not attributable to the Israelite Community.

" The curiosity of Europeans being only the

more excited from this narrative, as there still remained much to learn; at the instance of Souciet, who was compiling a large Work upon the Bible, the missionaries Gozani, Domenge, and Gaubil, were successively directed to procure additional particulars on the subject: which they did. Domenge sketched a plan of the synagogue; and Gaubil copied afresh the inscriptions upon its walls. Shortly after the last of these visits in 1723, the missionaries were expelled from that province by the Emperor Yongching.

"An effort was afterwards made by the celebrated Kennicott of Oxford, to obtain a collation of their Scriptures with our copies, when Sir F. Pigou, being on his way to Canton, carried out for him a printed Hebrew Bible of the Amsterdam edition; but the only result has been a letter, received in 1769 from a friend there, promising to exert himself for the purpose, and stating that the titular Bishop of the Province was willing to render him assistance.

"The learned Tychsen, upon two later occasions, in 1777 and 1779, forwarded letters to friends in Batavia, addressed to the synagogue of Kae-fung-foo; but no information has been returned as to their even having reached China.

"In 1815, the year previous to the last embassy from England to the Celestial Empire, some Jews of London had despatched a letter in Hebrew to Canton for this synagogue. It was conveyed thence by a travelling bookseller of the Ho-nan province. He delivered it at Kae-fung-foo to a person, whom he found to understand the letter perfectly, and who promised to answer it in a few days; but the bearer taking alarm at a rumour of civil war, left the place without waiting for the reply.

"The recent missionaries from England have learned nothing concerning this colony : only, in 1816, Dr. Morrison heard of them from a Mohammedan near Pe-king, as subsisting in Kae-fung-foo under their old name of *the Religion of cutting out the sinew :* an appellation so appropriately Jewish, that no other people than descendants of Jacob could even assign a reason for its origin, if they were to assume the name for any purpose"*.

Here a question will be raised : as to whether these indisputable *Hebrews* are *Jews* or *Israelites ;*

* Finn's Jews in China, chap. 1.

that is to say, whether they be emigrants of the Assyrian Captivity, or wanderers from Babylon of the Babylonian Captivity, or refugees from Jerusalem after the Roman Dispersion.

Mr. Finn pronounces them to be *Jews*, as contradistinguished from *Israelites*. Father Ricci, on the contrary, deemed them *Descendants of the Ten Tribes*, as contradistinguished from *Jews;* and supposed them to be a part of the Dispersion throughout the uttermost regions of the East, after the original deportation into Assyria and the Cities of the Medes.

His reasoning is precisely that which I should adopt; and I think it better than that of Mr. Finn, though absolute certainty may be justly pronounced unattainable.

It is based upon their total ignorance both of the name Jew and the name Jesus.

Had they been Jews either from Babylon or from Jerusalem, they could not have been ignorant of the very name of Jew: and, had they been Jews who emigrated in consequence of the Roman Dispersion, and after the crucifixion of our Lord, they must, like Jews in every other part of the world, have been familiarly acquainted both with the name and with the history of Jesus.

To confute this reasoning strikes me as no easy matter; and yet it is not the whole that may be said.

If these Hebrews were *Jews* as contradistinguished from *Israelites*, it is incredible, that they should have recollected and retained the name of ISRAELITES, while they had totally forgotten their special name of JEWS.

Accordingly, M. Renaudot, who is no light authority, though his Work does not appear in the list of Books consulted by Mr. Finn, subscribes to the opinion of Ricci. At least, he states, that Ricci's supposition, as to these Israelites being a fragment of the Ten Tribes deported by Shalmaneser, *does not seem to be much out of the way.*

Renaudot's account of the discovery of this Israelitish Community is the same as that given by Mr. Finn. But in one point there is, *numerically*, a very material difference. Mr. Finn describes the Hebrew visitor of Ricci as stating, that, in his native city, there were ten or twelve families of Israelites: but Renaudot makes him say, that, in that same city, there were ten or twelve *thousand* Israelitic families. Whether this be a case of omission or of interpolation, as respects the important word *thousand*, I have no means of deciding.

The supposition that these Hebrews are Israelites by no means interferes with the belief, that the Jews, distinctively so called, abound in Asia. This seems, in some degree, to have shaken Renaudot in his approbation of Ricci's argument : for he subsequently employs much the same reasoning to prove them to be Jews, which Mr. Finn has used, and which I have ventured to pronounce inconclusive. But I can see no warrant in the wide dispersion of the Jews for the change, or at least the modification of his first expressed opinion. The question solely respects the nationality of those Hebrews, to whose Community the visitor of Ricci belonged : and, however numerous the Jews might be throughout Asia, still the testimony remains unaffected, that Ricci's visitor called himself an *Israelite*, and was alike ignorant of the name both of JEW and of JESUS. Nor can it be said, that, although the name of JEW is familiar to *us*, it was not so, as used contradistinctively to the name of ISRAELITE, to the children of Judah themselves after their return from Babylon. For the perfect familiarity of the name, which seems, in fact, to have superseded that of *Israelite*, we need only turn to the New Testament; and, if we ask for more ancient evidence, we have it in the contemptuous question of Sanballat, in the day of the restoration from Babylon, *What do these feeble* Jews? Yet, if the Hebrews of China be Jews as contradistinguished from Israelites, they must not only have forgotten their own long familiar designation, but must also have assumed another designation which for many centuries had been laid aside*.

The fact of the wide dispersion of the proper Jews throughout Asia, I consider of vital importance to the due accomplishment of Prophecy.

It is again and again foretold, that Israel and Judah will be restored simultaneously, and that, when restored, they will jointly form a single kingdom in the land of their forefathers†.

Accordingly, when the Lord shall assemble the outcasts of Israel, and gather together the yet more widely dispersed of Judah from the four corners of the earth, the various lands, out of which the remnants of his people will be reco-

---

* Renaudot's Inquiry concerning the Jews discovered in China, p. 183–199.

† Jos. xi. 11–16. Jer. xxiii. 1–8. Ezek. xxxvii. 15–28.

vered, Jews as well as Israelites, are specified to
be Assyria, Egypt, Pathros, Cush, Elam, Shinar,
Hamath, and the Islands of the Sea, or the
Maritime Regions of Europe in the West. Of
these, Assyria is specially the land of the deportation of the Ten Tribes: but this does not
shut out other lands, into which they may have
emigrated, and in which therefore they may be
existing conjointly with the Jews. Such an in-
termixture will of course prepare the way for a
simultaneous restoration, and will perfectly facilitate their final predicted union as a single people
in a single kingdom. There is, however, *this*
local distinction to be drawn. The Isles of the
Sea *exclusively* refer to the Dispersion of Judah;
and, *specially* to facilitate the return of this division, the figurative tongue of the Egyptian Sea is
dried up, while the mystic Euphrates is smitten
into seven streams to prepare a way for the exiles
from the East. I have used the word *exclusively*,
because it is morally certain, that none of the
Israelites of the Ten Tribes migrated from Assyria into Europe. At that time, namely, in the
year A.C. 724, and the following years, Europe
was in a state of barbarism: the natural consequence, therefore, would be, that the various

emigrations of the Israelites from Assyria would be exclusively into the regions of eastern and southern Asia; for none would emigrate into a barbarous land, when they had civilised lands in their immediate reach. But the Jews, as our Lord foretold, have been led away captive into *all* nations. Hence we must look for *them* in the West, as well as in the East and the South. Under these circumstances, it is quite easy to conceive, that, when the Israelites shall be restored, the Jews will also be restored simultaneously out of the various regions of the East, as well as particularly and specially out of Europe and Africa; for the Downfall of Turkey and the Overthrow of the Egyptian Kingdom will alike prepare the way of God's ancient people, in both branches, from the East and from the West.

On this subject, I have gone into a greater length than I should otherwise have done, on account of the remarkable movement which now agitates China. It may justly be called one of the most extraordinary of the numerous signs of the times, even marvellous in the present day as those signs are; signs, which have now been multiplying upon us with a fearful profusion for more than sixty years. If this movement should

H

proceed to a successful termination, and if Christianity should become the national religion of the
long hermetically-sealed Chinese Empire, with its
population of more than three hundred millions,
it cannot but have a mighty influence both on
the Restoration and the Conversion of the Ten
Tribes, while it will equally promote the simultaneous Restoration and Conversion of the Jews
properly so called. Scriptural Chronology, combined with Historical Fact, shows, that these
great events cannot be very far distant. As we
have now an English Bishop and an English
Ecclesiastical Establishment in what was recently
a Chinese Island, and as, moreover, we have free
legal access to various ports on the long-extended
coast of China, an inquiry into these matters, if
practicable, would be highly desirable.

Sherburn House, Aug. 22, 1853.

———

Since this was written, I have perused a very
curious letter, printed at length in the "Morning
Herald," of Aug. 27, touching the Chinese
Movement.

Happily, as might be expected from its origination, the Christianity of these new religionists

has not in it a vestige of Popery. It is a singular mixture of Truth and Falsehood; the Falsehood, springing rather from defects of information, than from any perversion of the knowledge which had been received. Most remarkably, (may we not say *providentially*, likewise?) the whole Religious Movement seems to have originated from a Tract, or rather a Collection of Tracts, written or compiled by a Chinese Christian, named *Leang A-fah*. The Collection is entitled *Good Words to admonish the Age*. Its writer or compiler is still alive. He was baptized at Malacca, in the year 1816, by Dr. Milne; and he still continues abundant in labours, connectedly with Dr. Hobson's operations in Canton. Hence we cannot wonder that the Movement should be untainted by Popish Superstition. A-feh was the first convert made by Protestant Missions; and, through him, is thus communicated a potent influence on the mind of the leader, which, like a fire, has already extended to tens of thousands, and which may shortly spread over the whole of this vast and thickly-peopled Empire.

The probability seems to be, that, when more fully instructed, the Chinese of the Movement will become sound and decided Protestants. They already acknowledge one sole God, Jehovah, revering him in Three Persons : and idols of every description they hack to pieces and demolish. It does not appear, whether as yet they have come in contact with the worshipped images of Popish idolaters ; but those of the kindred superstition of Buddha, the similarity of which to Romanism has been felt and acknowledged by the Papists themselves, they have relentlessly destroyed in such numbers, that the fragments of these wooden gods, intermixed with gigantic images of Buddha, covered the surface of the whole river of Nankin. No doubt, they will serve the tawdry Madonnas and Bambinos of the Pope's religion in the same manner, when they come in their way ; for they seem to be thorough-going iconoclasts.

The Christian World may well look out with impatience and anxiety for further details.

Aug. 29, 1853.

London :—Printed by G. BARCLAY, Castle St. Leicester Sq.

BOSWORTH'S LITERATURE FOR THE PEOPLE.

No. 1.

A SUMMER CRUISE IN THE MEDITERRANEAN ON BOARD AN AMERICAN FRIGATE.

BY N. PARKER WILLIS.

Square fcap. 8vo. well printed, and containing upwards of 300 pages, 1s. 6d. sewed and 2s. cloth.

No. 2.

MR. CARLYLE ON SLAVERY.
Occasional Discourse on the Nigger Question.

COMMUNICATED BY T. CARLYLE.

Square fcap. 8vo. price 6d.

No. 3.

THE SPECTATOR.
With Biographical and Critical Preface and Notes.

New Edition in four well-printed vols. square fcap. 8vo. sewed, each, 2s. 6d.; or cloth, 3s.; or in 20 parts, each containing 96 pages, price 6d.   Part I. is now ready, and Vol. I. will be published in a few days.

₊ The Publisher intends to issue immediately a Series of Standard and Interesting Works, in the same style as the present volumes, in order to meet the rapidly-increasing demand for "Good Literature at a Low Price."

LONDON :
THOMAS BOSWORTH, 215 REGENT STREET.